# ENACTMENT: GREEK TRAGEDY

Other books by Albert Cook

THE DARK VOYAGE AND THE GOLDEN MEAN

THE MEANING OF FICTION

OEDIPUS REX: A MIRROR FOR GREEK DRAMA

PROGRESSIONS (poems)

THE ODYSSEY (verse translation)

THE CLASSIC LINE: A STUDY IN EPIC POETRY

PRISMS: STUDIES IN MODERN LITERATURE

THE ROOT OF THE THING: THE BOOK OF JOB AND
    THE SONG OF SONGS

THE CHARGES (poems)

MIDWAY (poems)

# ENACTMENT: GREEK TRAGEDY

## ALBERT COOK

THE **SWALLOW PRESS** INC.

CHICAGO

Published by

The Swallow Press Incorporated
1139 South Wabash Avenue
Chicago, Illinois 60605


This book is printed on 100% recycled paper.



ISBN 0–8040–0539–7
LIBRARY OF CONGRESS CATALOG CARD NUMBER 78–153076

for   Barbara and Michael Roemer

# CONTENTS

# PREFACE

How does one extend a theoretical statement about literature enough beyond formal analysis to broach literature's concern about life? This problem is a special case of the general problem of balancing what one includes in any verbal statement whatever. I feel I am off-balance between the theory that preponderates in the first section of this book and the formal analysis that dominates the second section. It may be that to handle materials of a certain weight one must be off-balance. For whatever it is worth, I cannot get any farther towards dispensing with the formal analyses, though I value them only for their theoretical bearing; that is, for their power to read the larger implications of a play.

My hope, in other words, is to make individual plays comment on Greek tragedy, in order to proceed towards having drama make a comment about life.

This is the first in a series of three studies. The second, to follow almost at once, *French Tragedy/the Power of Enactment*, will closely parallel the first. The third, about Shakespeare and his contemporaries, will not appear for some time; it may differ considerably from the others.

In this undertaking I have had much institutional support and individual help. It was begun during an invigorating fellowship year at the Center for Advanced Study in the Behavioral Sciences, at Palo Alto, developed on summer grants from the State University of New York and the American Council of Learned Societies, and completed (the first and second studies) on a Guggenheim Fellowship. A month with the fine library and the astute company at the Fondation Hardt in Geneva allowed me to solidify my project at a crucial stage.

Presenting drafts of some of this material to the Colloquium, the faculty course at the State University of Buffalo, enabled me to rethink many questions in stimulating dialogue with my colleagues, especially

Lionel Abel, Raymond Federman, Irving Feldman, Mac Hammond, Norman Holland, Joseph Riddel, Aaron Rosen, and William Sylvester. Besides these, C. L. Barber and René Girard sustained this stimulation in their own continuation of the Colloquium by centering it on questions that happened to be related to the ones I have been asking here. All of these read some parts of this book and made helpful comments. Charles Segal was kind enough to turn his customarily thorough and perceptive attention to my entire manuscript and to make suggestions which ranged from improvements (or corrections) of detail to basic structural recommendations.

My research assistant Phillip Bodrock also made useful suggestions, in addition to organizing the notes. His successor, Clint Goodson, while helping to prepare the final manuscript, proposed a number of stylistic improvements that I have gratefully incorporated. For careful typing of a naggingly detailed text I am especially indebted to my secretary, Mary Ann Lewis.

In addition to their heartening encouragement for all my writings and their able editorial help, Durrett Wagner and Michael Anania of the Swallow Press have sharpened the form of this book by insisting that it appear as a coherent unit by itself.

As always, I am profoundly indebted to my wife Carol in ways that it is not too fulsome to say "beggar description."

# INTRODUCTION

Every play is a happening, an event programmed for a particular place at a particular time. If the play succeeds, it transforms its time-bound and space-rooted significations, a fact which obliges the viewer to account both for the transformation and for the given significations themselves, not an easy double task. In the case of Greek tragedy, for example, it will not do simply to point out that *Oedipus Rex* begins with a plague similar to the one that had just afflicted Athens, or that much of Sophocles and most of Euripides was written under the shadow of war.

The function of war's stress is obvious in the plays but not patent. The Athenians were "politically," as we would say, imperialistic, as well as culturally so, and their relationship to every other city in the Hellenic world, to every regional group of city-states, remained in problematic tension through most of the time the plays were being produced. There was a specific historical pressure, as well as a general social condition, that brought the city into the daylight (I had almost written "limelight") of the dramatic performance. Once the Peloponnesian War got under way, this tension expressed itself in the uncertainty, a matter of life and death, about alliances for or against the Athens where the plays were performed. The whole question of each city's loyalties in the war that divided all Greece is classified by Thucydides as a *kindunos*, a risk or danger, and not as *bebaios*, a stable factor. Every allied city stood in countertension to every other city in its region, whether for or against Athens. And the world was too small to allow for anything so simple as a domino effect: a change in one point of the network was felt complexly throughout the whole. Behind every play produced, perhaps even before the outbreak of the war, the legendary name of a city like Thebes or Corinth or Argos had to echo (how could it not?) with its name in the present world of the political forces to which the spectator was very vividly subjected.

1

The audience of *Oedipus Rex* had lived through two devastating invasions into Attica, the first during the summer of 431, all the way to the boundary of Eleusis and Athens, and the second the following year, and then suffered the terrible plague which they connected with the invasions.[1] These people could surely not have heard the name Thebes or Corinth in *Oedipus Rex* without being reminded that a Theban and a Corinthian contingent had been among the invaders. Nor could they even celebrate without some hint of subsistent defiance, their own ritual connections to neighboring Troezen in the *Hippolytus* a few years later without being reminded that Troezen[2] had been among the places ravaged by the invaders. The distant Panhellenic associations, which assert their durability in the permanence of the myth, must be taken to redirect, and so to weaken, the close, hostile associations with Thebes and Corinth, between which Athens is situated. Thus *Oedipus Rex* is transpolitical and renders in the charged wartime space what it also suggests in time, the likeness of Oedipus Tyrannos[3] to that city permuted against the difference between tyranny and democracy.

The points of political preoccupation might be shared between tragedian and historian explicitly, and Finley[4] demonstrates some of the congruences between the events of Thucydides' account and the events of some tragedies: "The first debate . . . that between the Corcyreans and Corinthians, turns on the same conflict between expedience and justice [as does] the *Medea*." "Antiphon expresses views almost identical with those of the Nurse in the *Hippolytus*." "Menelaus in *Ajax* (1073–80) and Creon in *Antigone* (666–76) . . . demand obedience to the state on the exact grounds expressed [by Archidamas in the Corcyrean dialogue]."

The playwrights early abandoned the explicit treatment of political subjects, of which our sole surviving example is the *Persians* of Aeschylus, a celebration of the victory of Salamis through the distorting mirror of the barbarian side. The *Phoenissae* and the *Milesians* of Phrynichus are the only two titles we have which indicate an explicitly political subject.[5] And in the tetralogy where the *Persians* occurs, it is juxtaposed in ways we cannot reconstruct with the mythological subjects of the *Phineus*, the *Glaucus*, and the *Prometheus Firelighter*.

It is either platitudinous or inconsequential to be content with ascribing the profound disturbances of imaginative works to generating disturbances in the outside world, and the Peloponnesian War, which provides the circumstances for the civic disintegrations in Euripides' plays, does not provide a full explanation for them (or else, to revive an old point, we should be content with studying Thucydides by himself). Yet the connection will stand, generally as Arrowsmith traces it[6] in the *Medea*, and more specifically in that play because Corinth, the city Medea flouts after it has flouted her, was on the Spartan side in the war,[7] a fact that, again, has to be included in the sign system of references for an audience seeing the play at the beginning of the war. Medea escapes to Athens, and that fact has to mitigate the play's sense of her monstrosity. She begins as a woman wronged, and the tension between her justification and her atrocity finds its geographical dimension in her being a Greek-descended barbarian princess wronged by an enemy of Athens and rescued by an Athenian king.

That king, Aigeus, served as the protagonist of lost plays by both Sophocles and Euripides. Erechtheus, too, and Theseus, as well as Athene herself, occur frequently as characters in the plays, bringing the legendary past of the *polis* to bear on a plot enacted before its assembled representatives.

The pressure of the war on Euripides is most apparent, and most easily accounted for, when he succumbs to jingoism. In the *Children of Heracles* the descendants of the hero seek refuge in the small town of Marathon (or in the region, as Zuntz[8] maintains), a dependency of Athens in legend, in history the site of a famous victory, and at the time of the Peloponnesian war a Spartan ally. An emissary from Heracles' enemy, Erystheus, demands that the little state return the suppliants to Argos, a city powerful in legend but by this time reduced to dependency on the main antagonists and waveringly supporting Sparta in an attempt to placate both sides.[9] Resisted by Theseus's son Demophon, they attack and lose, thanks to a voluntary sacrifice of Heracles' daughter Macaria, a primitive reversion at the center of the play in the impasse Iolaus bemoans when she is taken away:

"A greater ruin, or else these conditions." (607)

In the battle Erystheus is captured, and the Athenians, exemplary upholders of the martial code toward prisoners, will not at first let him be executed. Once buried, however, he will be friendly to Athens and hostile to his own Argives (1030–45), and he is led off somewhat willingly to an execution the Athenians have both ways—an ending to which perhaps some irony clings, but not enough.

"The city is gone", ($\pi \acute{o}\lambda \iota \varsigma$ $\mu \grave{\epsilon}\nu$ $o \check{\iota}\chi \epsilon \tau \alpha \iota$, 14) Iolaus proclaims in the prologue, and the word *polis* occurs twenty-five times in the play.

In the *Suppliants*, too, legendary descendants act out an exemplum for the inheritors of legend. The mothers of the Argives who attacked Thebes under Polyneices seek the aid of Athens for recovering the bodies of the fallen heroes. In that legendary past, two present forces against Athens, the neutral Argives and the Thebans, an enemy as a member of the Boeotian League, were enemies of each other. The honorable resolution of this last strand to the Gordian knot of the Theban legend is again Athens; and though powerful arguments are martialled to keep Theseus from doing the decent thing, his mother Aithra brings him round.

The ensuing battle between Thebes and Athens is presented as a contest between tyranny and democracy, but the victorious Theseus magnanimously refrains from sacking the city. After the strange interlude of Evadne's immolation on her husband's funeral pyre, and her father's consequent despair, Athene gets Adrastus to swear that Argos will never attack Athens. She does, however, prophesy that Athens will one day sack Thebes.

In both of these plays Athens is doubled with a dependency, Marathon in the first and Eleusis in the second. And in both, the thematic unassimilability of the sacrificial or quasi-sacrificial immolation betrays the idealogical hardening of a *polis* ideal away from the profound and integral vision of the *Antigone*, the *Oedipus at Colonus*, or even the *Trojan Women*. Three orders of citizens ($\pi o \lambda \acute{\iota} \tau \omega \nu$, *Suppliants*, 238) are outlined in Theseus's argument with Adrastus (238–49): the blest who always desire more, the have-nots who are awesomely managing ($\delta \epsilon \iota \nu o \grave{\iota}$ $\nu \acute{\epsilon}\mu o \nu \tau \epsilon \varsigma$, 241) a full share of grudge against those who have, and the third kind, in between, that "saves cities" ($\sigma \acute{\omega}\zeta \epsilon \iota$ $\pi \acute{o}\lambda \epsilon \iota \varsigma$, 244) by preserving order ($\kappa \acute{o}\sigma \mu o \nu$, 245). But categorization implies, here, inadequacy, and Theseus elects to preserve order by refusing to help Adrastus. The emotional appeal of his mother subverts all this rationale, presumably leaving Athens unalterably in the third and best category of cities. Still, in the more unified plays, rationale and emotion are brought together through the special achieved enactment of the myth that here is dissolved to the advantage of jingoistic point-making.

The central activity of democratic life in the Athenian *polis*, open debate on questions of policy, remains a feature of all tragic plays, an analogy in the represented dialogue with the political process, as the performance of the play was an element of public religious worship. These two dimensions, the political and the religious, connected in the best plays, were connected in the *polis* as well; as Vernant says,[10] every magistracy retains a sacral character.

Euripides later avoids these political pressures by retreating to the ground of the theological problems that in the *Ion* he represents as prior to the polity, since Ion is the eponymous ancestor of those Ionians who settled Athens—an obscure legend that he brings into the light—and since the question of his rule over Athens is settled on religious and familial, rather than on political grounds.

Though Euripides wavered towards oversimplifying the *polis*, as Sophocles and Aeschylus did not—a point rendered by Aristophanes in the Alcibiades test of the *Frogs* (1422–36)—the wavering itself brought him to the threshold of other problems. The basis of intellectual debate, dangerously split from the emotions of Theseus in the first half of the *Suppliants*, enters in the *Bacchae* and the *Ion* into dynamic interrelation with a deep emotional ambivalence, so riddling that the tragicomic moments there are themselves questioned. These plays go beyond the *polis*; yet, as always, they happen within it. They are public events, and their meanings, unlike those of our plays, are brought back through the context of the unique performance to the *polis* itself, even though the *polis* may be declining irreversibly towards the annihilation of a total war.

2

A play enacts. In doing so it not only makes a statement; it also creates an effect, in a given context, on an idealized (Greek) spectator. The effect unites with the statement, as the mythos with the logos.

A play, statement and effect taken together, is a linguistic act. It sets up an interaction between its construct of verbal acts and its construct of silent acts. Both kinds of acts, indeed, imply expectation in the audience. Both are assimilable to what J. L. Austin[11] calls "performatives," statements in language designed not to assert truth but to bring about some result. Or, to use Jakobson's terms, they center on the addressee as "conative."

Now since all statements do exist in some context of expectation and since, as Austin[12] says, "the total speech act in the total speech situation is the *only actual* phenomenon which, in the last resort, we are engaged in elucidating," then all statements ultimately involve the addressee, whatever their schematic relation to speaker, code, message, contact, or referent. All statements are to some degree "performative" and "conative," when taken in context. And dramatic statements, plays, fairly shout to be taken in context, since the theater where they are presented constitutes a context whose features have become formalized.

When we approach a particular formal context for the Greek drama, we have to ascertain the external features of the context, especially the political history, as well as the internal features, the linguistic statement of the play itself.

Stressing a particular significance, be it political or social, involves the risk of settling for one special meaning of a particular play. So Rosenmeyer[13] offers the question of time as the locus of whatever mystery the *Ajax* enacts. Hegel[14] wants the *Antigone* not just to illustrate but to expound his dialectic. Verrall[15] extrapolates the myth-questioning in *Alcestis* and *Ion* and sets it up as a myth-refutation. For Freud[16] the *Oedipus* "grips" the spectator because it embodies the one unvarying pattern of his unconscious life. Where not oversimplifying, the good commentators have tended to look too exclusively at the context—at the fact that tragedy occurs during a kind of religious festival—or too exclusively at the separable "constative" statements in the play, as Jebb[17] does when he ponders whether in his last speech Ajax is intending to deceive his auditors or level with them (actually, in my opinion, both are the case, and yet we should not avail ourselves of the convenient term "ambiguity" as a way of preventing ourselves from apprehending what this doubled time-view entails). Or again, Errandonea[18] creates astute ratiocinative bridges among Ajax's four main speeches as a way of addressing the same problem raised by Jebb, but these bridges hang over an abyss somewhat shallower than the one spanned by the play.

Beyond such close readings, there are three overlapping areas of help, of which we might avail ourselves, but they cover only so much; they resolve special questions, but do not constitute any general scheme for Greek drama. Still, they are constant in what they offer, and I should like to dwell on them not so much to dismiss them as to weigh or more precisely to consider how they might help us. These are the formal, or Aristotelian; the psychological, or Freudian; and the myth-analytic in its most schematic form, or Straussian.

To take Aristotle first, he offers us, of course, an abundance of precious historical information. And he offers us also some hard distinctions about particular plays and about literature in general. His thoughts on beginning, middle, and end, on simple and complex plots, on the plot as the soul of the action, remain lodestones for critical thought everywhere. And his four classes (*eide*, form-types) of tragedy are almost equally apposite and puzzling. When, for example, he classifies the *Ajax* under plays that are *pathetike*, involving passive suffering rather than action, we may note with interest that *pathos* and *pathe* occur at least six times in the *Ajax*, a comparatively high incidence.[19] On the other hand, the word *ponos*, struggle or labor, occurs at least thirteen times and is coded more complexly into the play. *Ponos* can be set against *pathos* as easily as the two can be reconciled.

Now Aristotle did not say Sophocles's *Ajax* was *pathetike*;[20] he said that Ajaxes in general were, or we may presume prescriptively had to be, "the pathetic as *Ajaxes* are", (ὅσον ὁί τε Αἴαντες), which implies that an Ajax play has got to be a certain way, have a certain *eidos* or form-type.

It is in the middle ground of prescriptions about groups of Greek plays in general that Aristotle is weakest, as valuable as are his particular *aperçus*, his historical information, and his general literary theory. *Hamartia*, in his discussion, offers an explanation in terms of "error" for afflictions which the actual plays, again and again, speak of as inexplicable, or else as subject to the general human rule that no life prospers throughout its full course. *Peripeteia* and *anagnorisis*, reversal and recognition, are serviceable general terms. It also illuminates the *Oedipus Rex* to say of it that there the *peripeteia* and the *anagnorisis* coincide.[21] But to say that ideally they should always so coincide, to use these terms in the middle ground of many other plays, is to suffer

Occam's razor. The categories get in our way; they will not explain.

Now this middle ground is the one we want to occupy, and I fear it is the ground Aristotle himself intended to occupy. To make sense of his categories, in so far as they pretend to define Greek tragedy, one should look for the most part not at Greek tragedy, but rather at the whole of the Aristotelian system. When he says that with the addition of the third actor, tragedy achieved its natural form, its *physis*,[22] we cannot question the remark as a historical attribution, but we may question the theory of it, in so far as that theory applies specifically to Greek tragedy. The remark, of course, is best understood not in the context of Aeschylus, Sophocles, and Euripides, but in the context of Aristotle's technical system. Not only *physis*, but *eidos* or form-type (a word with a Platonic history), and in fact "reversal" and "recognition" themselves, take on full meaning in the context of the *Metaphysics* and the *Ethics* and the *Organon*, as does Aristotle's theory of action. Else's book[23] succeeds in expounding that theory precisely by referring the *Poetics* to the full context of Aristotle. There is room for another book on the *Poetics* which would treat it as Cherniss's book does Aristotle and the Pre-Socratics. Cherniss[24] argues forcefully that because he always had his own system in mind, Aristotle's remarks about Parmenides, Empedocles, and others at the beginning of the *Physics* and the *Metaphysics* tell us more about the system than they do about his predecessors. If we look there for reliable statements about Parmenides and Empedocles, we will be misled. The book balancing the *Poetics* against its presumptive subject matter is one that ought to be written. I shall not write it, but to write it would be the only thorough way of demonstrating what I am here asserting. In the meantime, Aristotle is to be taken only in small doses, several hours apart, and by adults.

Freud[25] went to Greek tragedy for his model, which is not just the Oedipus myth but that myth in the hands of Sophocles. He compares the progress of the action in that play to the progress of a psychoanalysis. He explains the power of the play by its ability to engage the feelings of the spectator. He uses the verb *ergreifen*, to grip; he speaks of the spectator as *tief ergriffene*, and *ungerührt* when in modern plays, the spectator is unaroused. Here Freud has taken, perhaps, a small dose of Aristotle, who says that, in seeing a play, a catharsis is brought about,

a purifying of pity and terror.[26] I suggest that a prolonged consideration of what catharsis means will lead us, again, and not surprisingly,
back to Aristotle's system even more than it leads us to the history of
Greek cults, popular and esoteric. We will do much better to attend to
Freud, who provides, with interpretation to be sure, a usable schema
for the transaction effected on the emotions of a mass addressee, an
idealized audience, by that complex performative and conative statement, the play.

This first use of Freud, applying his terminology to the transaction
taking place across the orchestra boundary, will take us very far. It
provides a scheme and a vocabulary for what happens in the drama's
distancing of statement into visible others. A second use takes the
Freudian schemes as they come up in the mythos, applying them not
to the whole dramatic transaction across the actor-spectator line, but
rather to the dynamic of relations among the people on stage (which,
to be sure, gives us some of the syntax of the big performative statement). So common, indeed, is this use in our time, that a mere mention
of the facts will bring the scheme into place. Ajax, for example, has a
father, a son, and a wife, as well as a brother, and they come into his
talk more often than his mother does. He commits suicide on the sword,
and there is much talk about the sword, which he got from his enemy
Hector. Of all his gear, the sword is the sole thing he will not bequeath
to his son: he intends to take it to the underworld with him. If he
effectuates any deception, it all centers on the sword. Secretive he
certainly is, even toward his wife, who is a captive, a former noblewoman, who will become a slave if he dies. To kill himself, then, may
injure others, and especially his wife.

Should he want to injure women? the analyst asks. Or, did anybody
else in his past capture a noblewoman? Indeed yes. His father Telamon
left Salamis, his home, and went off to King Laomedon, where by
trickery he captured a noblewoman whom he made a slave, Hesione,
the mother of Teucer. The small boy Ajax may be imagined to have
registered this threatening sexual exploit of his father and later to have
repeated it. Where was Laomedon at the time? On that very road
where Ajax now stands, building the walls of the Troy that Ajax is
attacking because of still another sexual exploit. Teucer, the resultant
half-brother, becomes his other self, or his son does, and those are the
titles of the two lost plays of Sophocles' trilogy, the *Teucros* and the

*Eurysakes.* Suicide is a well-known danger in psychoanalysis, and from a depth-psychological point of view one could coordinate all the personal relations in the play around Ajax's self-castrating suicide. Not only would the relations of brother and wife, mother and father and son thereby come into focus, but so also would the relations of Ajax to Odysseus, Menelaus, and Agamemnon, and through them, to the Greeks and Trojans, enemies and friends, generally.

These Freudian patterns, while valid in themselves, constitute only part of the syntax of the total statement, and not even the central part. For the play deploys another syntax, not that of men and men, but that of men and gods; and the plane of Athene and Pan, Apollo and Artemis, is not resolved by psychoanalysing it; at least, not directly.

In the paralinguistic or translinguistic ordering of roles, mythic systems are strikingly deployed in Greek culture generally and particularly in tragic plays. In the *Ajax* there are several sets of terms; we have a set Greek/Trojan, interlocking with a set local/Panhellenic. A set man/Gods is expanded to include, as a kind of middle term, beast; giving man/beast. It is infinitely ignominious to confuse these categories, as Ajax has begun his ignominy by confusing the related category man/God, taking upon himself the responsibility which properly belongs to Athene. Calchas says of Ajax that he does not think in a human way (οὐ κατ' ἄνθωπου φρονῶν). So beasts are usually offerings, and that is one word applied by the play to these beasts. They are slaughtered neither as sacrifices in a man/God relationship because the beast has some totemic value in a beast/God set, nor as food to be eaten after being subjected to the *feu de cuisine* (the sacrificed thighs were sprinkled raw) in a proper set of the distinction man/beast.

Or again, in the *Suppliants* of Aeschylus, the Danaids, who are at once chorus and collective protagonist, have crossed the sea to be rescued by invoking an opposition Asia (Egypt)/Europe (Greece in the form of archaic Argos), a contrast insisted on throughout the play. They do this to avoid just the sort of forced marriage that Zeus, to whom they pray, committed upon their ancestor Io, in an opposition beast/God; and the memory, as their very prayer recapitulates it, connects the name of Io's offspring Epaphus with the word "touch" in a sexual sense, tying the past of the myth to the horror they will generate in the lost plays of the trilogy by killing those who marry them, including the descendants of Io. That itself introduces another under-lying–opposition, male/female; the opposition between blood kinship and marriage rules, the incest taboo which here is implicitly stronger for Greek than for Egyptian. The maze of this mythos is chargeable to Zeus, but it will take another trilogy, in which Io appears as a main character (and the only human in the play), to level the charge, the *Prometheus*. Meanwhile, between the two moments of impasse in the *Suppliants*, that of protection for the suppliant to which Pelasgus finally accedes and that of force from the sons of Aegyptus, to which he does not, the Danaids declare Zeus to be an infinite limit for human vision:

$$τί \ δὲ \ μέλλω \ φρένα \ Δίαν$$
$$καθορᾶν, \ ὄψιν \ ἄβυσσον;$$

How shall I scan the mind
Of Zeus, a sight-abyss?                    (1057–58)

In introducing interchanging sets of binary alternatives, along with what amounts to plus and minus valuations, I have moved not only into the area of anthropology generally, but specifically into that of Lévi-Strauss. Expanding out of these, in a separate set, we have for the *Ajax* the full complement of the *Structures elémentaires de la parenté*:[27] father–son, mother–son, father–mother: and then, instead of exoga-mous group, mother's brother–son, we have, in this firmly but newly assertive patriarchal society, a semislave for a mother. So instead of a relation between the mother's brother and the son, we have one be-tween son and father's brother, Teucer, who is doubly "plus" on the male side by being not just a father's brother, but a half-brother on the father's side only, in his relation to Eurysaces. And the same sort of pattern may be spelled out for the *Suppliants*.

Another part of the dramatic syntax, then, is offered by Lévi-Strauss, but to carry a play fully into his reticulations, to spell out series of homologous relations among these pairs, would be to part company with the cathartic transaction of performative language that a play constitutes. The algebra of Lévi-Strauss, for all its coordinated complexity, is one of intellect, not emotion; not just of intellect in its own structure—any formulation must be that—but in its referents.

So his Oedipus myth consists of types of overestimation of kinfolk paired against types of underestimation, and then types of mastering chthonic monsters paired against types of not mastering the chthonic deities. These alternations would never get us to the feeling underlying the sea image of "the surge of dread fate" (*Oedipus Rex*, 1527). Though his main analysis is directed to American Indian myth and not to Greek myth, we may apply his ideas by extrapolation. Lévi-Strauss would himself insist on the generalizable character of this evidence. Still, we have here not an algebra or calculus of the emotions, which Freud gives us, but a calculus of systematic thought in a "language to the second degree" whose laws belong to the ego-mind of a sort of transcendental and systematized *pensée sauvage*.

The logos of a play stands on a par with its mythos: the sweep of *Oedipus* resists assimilation to Lévi-Strauss or Freud or Aristotle. Through inventing what it objectifies on stage, a tragedy transforms all the significations it includes, as a liturgical presentation does not. Even the Mass does not comment on what it presents.

True drama, however, comments as it presents: presentation is commentary, and vice versa.

All the various types of fertility ritual which Theodor Gaster[28] finds in Ugaritic and other presentational texts are merely liturgical, and therefore subliterary. An anthropological or theological comment would theoretically exhaust them. But a literary work exists modally on a par with comments about it.

A seasonal ritual is merely cyclic. A Greek play, without breaking the cycle, expands it beyond recognition. Without getting into the moot question of origins, one may thank Gilbert Murray for noticing, as an underlying significative sequence in the Greek drama, a comparable fertility ritual:

> To sum up, we find that the tragedies of Euripides usually end with a Theophany of a markedly formal and ritual character, closely suiting our conception of the Sacer Ludus of Dionysus, as daimon of the Year-Cycle of death and rebirth; further, that in those tragedies which do not end in a confessed Theophany there are at any rate curious resemblances to the typical Theophany-form; furthermore...

> Aeschylus (shows) . . . a Theophany of a similar sort . . . .
> About Sophocles . . . the indications are not at all incon-
> sistent with the above results.[29]

It is the transformation of this signification series, not its presence, on which the drama hinges. Murray's evidence for the presence of Sacer Ludus under tragic plays will stand up in the face of any sub-tractions of Dionysus from pre-Aeschylean theatrical forms. Yet the anthropological fact, once established, leaves, as always, the more crucial question of how this signification is transformed. What happens to this type-mythos when it is cast in the form of a particular myth, set out before an audience, and clothed in a logos series whose own significations are slanted by various meters?

I

# Chapter One: MYTHOS

## 1

The universe of myth, to demythologize it, is a universe of the dynamized emotions. Zeus is god of the gladdeningly bright or the awesomely dark sky; Dionysus stirs up darkness in the light; Apollo, in lighting and curing, brings jubilation and calm. The hidden powers of emotion have drawn those of modern times who invent or resurrect myth, as Nietzche and Wagner, Blake and Goethe. In primacy of feeling the sterile anger of Urizen resembles the fertile anger of Los. Blake's universe geometrizes feelings where *Gefühl ist alles*, where *die Mutter* are not just muttered as in *Faust*, but cartwheel through *zoas* of variegated embodiment. For Freud, the body itself is merely an instrument on which the unconscious plays emotional music in the key signatures of a mythic Oedipus or his imperfect female counterparts. Ranging for other myths, Jung splits the clefs by doubling the man with his feminine opposite, the anima within him, and the woman with her own internal masculine animus. The history of consciousness unfolds a mythic counterpart to emotions in realized time.

Freud offers a fully consistent dynamic of interaction within the psyche between "other" forces, the third-personal *Es* or *Id*, as it manages, and in turn is managed by, a conscious first-person I. Greek thought locates the "other" in the *Umwelt*, not in the *Innenwelt*, but otherwise the dynamic between unconscious and conscious, or between emotion and ratiocinative construct, between the general force behind human acts and the particular manifestation, between type and fact, is schematized into a story, a myth. In this sense, as Cassirer[1] points out, the myth, like the performative statement of Austin, is not subject to the category truth-falsehood. It is a system of relations in context. From Freud's perspective, however, these relations are emotional ones, not intellectual ones; and bringing them to consciousness implies an emotional transaction, the transference. This is analogous to the dramatic transaction in certain ways: it carries emotion over from one place to another *(übertragen)*; the Freudian motto, *Wo Es war soll Ich werden* (where Id was there shall ego be), will serve well as a motto for Greek tragedy, always allowing the self to expand beyond clinical blank or construct.

Depth analysis, by relating personal emotion to the nucleus of mythic pattern happenings, preserves the character of emotion while standing aside from it, as other translations of emotion into intellect fail to do. All emotion may well have a physiological correlative,[2] but a graph of physiological and chemical reactions has lost the character of the emotion: in such accounts, emotion has not just been translated into conceptual signs; it has been sacrificed to them, and its urgency disappears, or is made too automatic. So for other translations, including those of emotion into measurements of space or time:[3] such graphable dimensions as that affection signals advantageous closeness, in measurable space, and aggression, a disadvantageous closeness, may offer a complete measurement also for what advantage is. Still, this dimension loses the unitary sense of pattern; it is all of the measured moment, neutralized. Finally, it cannot account for the history of an emotion, or the force of one in relation to others. In failing to be unitary, such analyses also fail to be typical. They fail to deal with the proper type or countervailing types that depth analysis retains and in retaining, manages. This a successful dramatic enactment does.

Dramatic presentation, moreover, transcends the emotion while preserving it: by the mighty sleights that compel our attention, it escapes that seemingly inescapable condition of loss. Oedipus Rex, who enacts before us in the play all the actuality of his myth, stands at a dead center of that myth while enacting it; he is thus the only man in the world without an Oedipus complex,[4] because he works his way through the obsessions of all other men by enacting them. He faces knowing them, as Sophocles dramatizes it, for in the play it has all happened already, and Oedipus may at any point listen to Tiresias or Jocasta and turn away from his past:

> Already many mortals in their dreams
> Have shared their mother's bed. But he who counts
> This dream as nothing, easiest bears his life.          (981–83)

By locating emotion in some series of events—historical as a time-bound series, eternal in its typicality—and by objectifying it in a prime set of transcendent agents, the myth assures, through all the instabilities and arbitrariness of the relation between emotion and intellect, an indissoluble connection between them. "A completed demythologization," Adorno says, "reduces transcendence wholly to the abstraction, the concept."[5] The myth also makes an ultimate of its transcendence; it is the beyond, and beyond its universe of emotions there is nothing conceivable. Gods and heroes, or divine animals and heroic people, embody the transcendences that orchestrate their actions.

Under the relations it deploys, Cassirer says, lies the stuff of myth.[6] The relational calculus in myth expounded by Lévi-Strauss is at the service of the transcendence, and it is thus possible to reinvest his entire abstract system back into the transcendence ("participation mystique") of the Lévi-Bruhl he seems silently to believe he is refuting. The intellect remains ultimately at the service of the transcendent emotion, the logos of the mythos, in the order of society as in the order of a social enactment, a Greek play.

As Whorf follows Cassirer in asserting, the logos of a language embodies deployments which amount to an implied metaphysical system, a "myth" in Cassirer's sense of a symbolic form. But the myths, properly speaking, of a culture, those for which it finds proper names, in Lévi-Strauss's demonstration,[7] are a second language, still another code within which the order or priority between intellect (sign) and emotion (feeling with the sign) are reversed. The ordinary language—though like all human phenomena it may be analyzed as a sublimation of unconscious (oral) cathexes—is first an ordering of abstract signs, of conceptual relations, to referents and to each other. It then adds to these the emotional implications of word association and intonational pattern. In a myth the figure of animal or god stands first as an object or cause of the transcendent emotions, to which the emotion of awe may be superadded. These figures are then combined through sets of relations in the binary disposition of events in the series, or "mythemes" in Lévi-Strauss's terms.[8] Thus one may see the unit to be the object, "Cadmus," for example, or "Oedipus," or "Sphinx," or "Tiresias," in which the emotions are invested, and not the event, which enters into intellectual relations. Lévi-Strauss, to the end of striking illumination, inverts this accepted order of myth because he wishes to stress the importance of the conceptual relations. He achieves this admirable aim, without at all demonstrating the primacy of these relations, though he creates an illusion of doing so by his displacement of the figure from the center of analysis in favor of event (so that the figure, of jaguar or opossum or tobacco or honey, becomes a locus of an event series, a mathematicized f-function). When he says[9] that he is moving from structure to process, he does not say how he had already moved from figure to structure, though of course his method implies breaking the (emotional) Gestalt of a figure into the (conceptual) relations of a structure, by dividing into separate events what the figure unites. Of course, figure and structure and process differ only in their angle of connection; they refer to the "same" myth—except that the figure, for all its translatability into structure or process, holds the mythic primacy of a unifying name.

The deployment of several patterns with the staple emotional association of meters and modes never seems disunifying in Greek drama, because the action itself is solidly grounded on mythical figures who appear either in one mass (the chorus) or in a group where the speakers can never exceed three.

The myth explains the mystery of ultimate forces by preserving the mystery in figures. The play reenacts the myth, on the stipulated ground of service to the embracing mythical figure of Dionysus, and it heightens explanation by reinvoking the mystery it is constructed to explain.


The figures of myth, gods and beasts and persons, are themselves relational, not only to each other, but to the events in actual life that they designate. To classify is to relate. The particular, or the unique individual, would be unknowable if it were not compounded of features which gave it membership in a class; an individual is a transcendent congeries of general attributes.

In Freud's reading of the unconscious, any unique person, through the mythic typification of his emotions, identifies himself as combining Mother and Father in a particular way. He meets other unique people by throwing onto them, whether in a self-realizing or a self-defeating way, the shadows of ambivalent love–hate toward these two figures. So the myth allows for the particular and the general to come together.

The myth, by thus generalizing, gives an immediate meaning to the fact, without the intermediation of language or other abstract patternings of thought. The doubling of not being the self (but rather the Son) generalizes a person into the possibility of being himself. In this sense, the invention of make-believe, which Snell[10] asserts has tragedy "detach itself from the pressure of reality," does not just make the Greek drama "*play*"; as a doubling, it embodies, through the emotional series of responses in the spectator (pity and terror), a transposition of logos into mythos, as well as the other way around. And finally it is the mythos that the logos is about, all the particulars are referrable to that generality. Moreover, the play remains, in the complex modalities of its utterance, an act of worship to Dionysus; its artistic features do not make it the kind of "work of art" which post-Industrialization aesthetics would have it be, and which Snell, with Kitto, reads back into Greece.[11]

The fact of feeling comes into its own through the pattern of the enacted myth. The emotion, in being typified, is known by being generalized; a person has not some terrible seizure, but an access of Aphrodite. The logos, in the *Hippolytus* or the *Andromache*, may build evocations out of that problematic mythos without either resolving the problem or dissolving the myth. Emotion, as a force, flows at particular moments. The myth typifies the force by generalizing the moments with a figure and a story.

One might go still further to mythologize myth, or rather to underscore the generalizing power it has, and call the type an archetype. This would hypostatize the fluidity, or rehypostatize it, since the myth had already done so. But Aphrodite has quite enough power: Euripides poses by reenactment what the force of that power may be. To speak of a Great Mother or a White Goddess would be, in a sense, to abrogate the possibility of listening to Euripides, by universalizing as a Great Mother what is already general in the figure of Aphrodite.

The spectator at a tragedy is rapt into union with those responding in a like way about him. He is individual, he is a general member of a group. The myth that relates the individual fact with the general pattern allows him to be one while being the other, to heighten his unique selfhood by attending to a calculated and patterned statement out there, in the general myth.[12] So, in the myth to begin with, the emotion attendant on bringing together the general of the group and the particular of the individual reconciles, as merely differences of emphasis, such seemingly contradictory assertions about the social function of myth as Freud's insistence on the individual on the one hand ("The myth is then the step by which the individual moves out of the psychology of the mass"[13]) and Lévi-Strauss's group-language definition of myth on the other ("Music exposes to the individual his own physiological roots; mythology, his social roots. One takes us in the guts, the other, if one may dare say it, 'in the group'."[14]). But the relation between individual and group in myth can be read either way, as the employment of music in the tragic representation of myths also may be taken to indicate.

Myth cosmologizes the emotions by providing for their forces, from far within the psyche to far without in the heavens, a set of nonlogical universals, to which the particulars of any human event may be referred without the fixity or even the mediation that conceptual coherence would call for. Much discussion of myth lacks full persuasiveness because it assumes, even while asserting the contrary, that myth is a kind of logical prelogic operating somehow on premises from which conclusions may be drawn, as of course our discussion about myth itself must do.

Myth, to begin with, presents an ambivalence: the sacred (sacer) is at once extremely holy and extremely foul. Aphrodite is dreadful and desirable. In the coupling and dividing impulses of the unconscious, identity is preserved by maintaining ambivalence towards the hate–love of the father and the love–hate of the mother. By preserving ambivalence, the myth violates the law of contraries, that a quality and its contrary cannot both be predicated of the same object at the same time. Clearly the logical intellect, whose activity can in turn be analyzed as a form of compulsive sublimation or aggression, can and will resolve contraries. But under the form of ambivalence, the contraries remain open to each other in the depths of the emotions, where hate can also include love for the same object at the same time, and without any logical trickery as without any logical resolution. The Dionysus of the *Bacchae* creates while he destroys, the Artemis of the *Hippolytus* implacably withdraws as she compassionately approaches, the invincible Zeus of the *Prometheus* may somehow be overcome. And the awe of Aeschylus, like the doubt of Euripides, retains of itself its own ambivalence.

Once out of the mythic sphere, ambivalence may be patiently analyzed, but it cannot be reproduced. Logic governs discourse, but not the immediacy of imaginative literature. Aeschylus or Beckett, Euripides or D. H. Lawrence, Sophocles or Henry James, may compellingly render ambivalence; but Norman O. Brown, in the discursive nets of *Life Against Death*,[15] gets caught up in asserting the, as it were Lutheran, principle of radical sickness (sinfulness), and at the same time in pleading for the contrary, the, as it were Pelagian, principle of radical health (the innocence of polymorphous perversity). But these contraries cannot be reconciled without recourse to the ground of myth—in Christian terms, to the reconciliation between the Redemption and the Fall, for which faith offers mediation and theology set after set of analyses (Brown, occupied in expounding a version of Freud, provides neither mediation nor analysis). This "paradox of the fortunate fall" finds representation in pretragic ritual, as Herbert Weisinger shows,[16] and it finds something more than representation, the transcendent enactment of understanding, in the great tragedies of Greece, and of the West generally, that preserve the ambivalence of the myth while in the process of addressing it and forcing it to yield transcendences.

The failure of profound effect in ephemeral literary work, or the short-circuiting of the sign-system in it, can be described in terms of a failure to manage the ambivalence of myth. Thus, bad romantic tales envision the mere horror of Aphrodite, or the mere delight, without blending the two. And even the sado-masochistic overemphases discussed by Mario Praz in *The Romantic Agony*[17] are found only in secondary works. The Luvah of Blake fuses horror and delight while "La Belle Dame sans Merci" overintoxicates itself in a mere horror which the Diotima of Hölderlin transcends. The incestuous Ushers, in their horror, are no match for Stendhal's Mathilde, Dostoievsky's Grushenka, or Tolstoi's Natasha. Popular literature, from James Fenimore Cooper to James Bond, must awaken the myth in order to have the kind of power that a Leslie Fiedler or a Richard Hoggart looks for in them; and yet they must leave the ambivalences asleep; they must remain, to stay with the usual confusing term, "sentimental." The category "popular literature" has its most pointed meaning with reference to the social structure of the world after industrialization. But the special semantic strategy that invokes myth without managing ambivalence may be found in all sorts of social structures, from the most primitive to the most civilized. In the matrix of Greek drama, the satyr play must have been a particularly unmanageable form; perhaps, indeed, that is why only one such play has come down to us (if we except fragments like the *Ichneutai* of Sophocles and a superbly enigmatic substitution for one in the *Alcestis* of Euripides). Euripides' *Cyclops* comes across not by reshaping the myth from the *Odyssey*, but by slavishly recapitulating the story, substituting sexual slapstick for any integral confrontation, bawdy or otherwise, of the sexual mysteries (as in line 169, and throughout). Among his other plays, even the *Rhesus*, for all the simplicity of its terror, does manage that by a kind of opposite in the person of Athene, and adds its small urgencies of commentary to Euripides' many meditations on war.

Greek tragedy sustains the ambivalence not just of one mythic figure, but of groups—of legendary persons enacting the play, or of gods dominating it: the *Hippolytus* brings Aphrodite into focus with her contrary, Artemis. Nietzsche, who hypostatized all Greek thought into drunkenness (Dionysus) and dream (Apollo), speaks of Greek tragedy as the "reconciliation of Apollonian and Dionysian power"[18]. The plays do freely invoke whole sets of gods.

2

The stuff of the emotions, to which the figures and events of the myth give substance, lends itself magisterially to these configurations of ambivalences. Since a given figure ideally preserves a myth's ambivalence, it may always be seen from this side or from that. There is always a point, then, at which one figure may be associated with another. Athene, as a severely masculine goddess, objectifies one function of her father, Zeus, from whose head she sprang full-grown. But she carries a shield, and so resembles Ares. As the tutelary goddess of a city (Athens), she exists in a repertoire of many tutelary deities. On her shield, moreover, she carries the severed head of the Gorgon, the aegis: that snaky head has been interpreted as the hysterical essence of femininity: the mother-with-a-penis split gorily into many writhing penis-snakes and killed to turn the beholder into stone. Castration here fuses with menstruation and with murder. In displacing her femininity from a castration, Athene may be said to resemble

Aphrodite, born from the foam of the sea-flung genitals of Ouranos.

Lévi-Strauss has demonstrated at great length and with peerless complexity how one must deploy the configurations of myth onto many planes, and he describes them as systems of coherent expansions from resolutions or mediations or intensifications of binary sets like culture and nature, earth and sky, land and water, sun and moon, down to the common sensory materials of seemingly insignificant nurture. One does not have to deploy the events of myth again, but just to take the figures, as above, to perform complex and variable operations. In the emotions, there is some plastic adaptability, which the fluidity of our feelings evidences, and which shows up further just in the adaptability of its force to the charge-manipulations of myth.

The emotion itself, then, in its adaptability, invites ambivalence; it may be said to exist only through ambivalence. And further, in Freudian terms, it may be said to exist only through myth: only by loving the Father and Mother as a Child can one love another person as a person.

As on our mortal earth, so in the timelessness of Olympus. If the myth is an emotional algebra of sorts that calculates the ambivalences into formulae, then myths are associable to one another, their functions translatable into one another: Athene into Zeus or Ares or Artemis or even Aphrodite. This possibility will hold for the events, on which Lévi-Strauss centers, as well as for the figures. By the transformational rules he provides, one can get from the sense of one event to the sense of another systematically, and one can also start anywhere, not only because the meaning of a given event or *mythème* arises precisely from its relation to other mythemes, but also because the senses are significant only within a total system where alternations and inversions of mythemes with each other guarantee the algebraic freedom which takes a particular shape in a given formulation or story.

Thus, one can take the force of the emotions by any mythic route, and Freud's great discovery is not the centrality of Oedipus but rather the generalizing power of myth in the unconscious to connect facts of the present to the pattern of the eternal past. He could as well have taken Hippolytus, courted by a present stepmother while his real father is away. Or he could have taken Perseus, who is set perilously loose from his real mother and threatened by his stepfather until he can kill the Gorgon by the use of a magic mirror, freeze the bad father-figure by brandishing the snaky head, and go off to rescue and marry a young girl chained, for reasons of sexual jealousy, to be the prey of still another monster. The *Oedipus Rex*, perhaps alone among Greek plays, resembles a psychoanalysis, as Freud said, not because of uniquely appropriate myth, but because of the step-by-step self-scrutiny of its literary structure. But any successful Greek play, and ultimately any compellingly rendered tale, derives its power from harnessing the strange stuff of which feelings are shaped and myths about them formed.

This strange stuff is so malleable to the patterning of myth that many thinkers have written as though the coherence of a pattern in a certain form were the final key to the nature of the underlying material. And the data, the anthropological facts, will support such interpretations; details will bend into coherence at the beck of the interpreter. As societies have been attentive to the sun, to successions in human authority and the seasons, to the central position of woman as a mediating figure between nature and culture (to follow Lévi-Strauss again): so it is possible to arrange all the myths of a society into one pattern around Max Müller's sun god or Frazer's hanged god or Robert Graves' white goddess version of Bachofen's *Das Mutterrecht*. The hero with a thousand faces has a single, adaptable heart. Neumann's Uroboros-Great Mother[19] who encompasses and transforms the self-asserting lover can be translated into Graves' white goddess loving the devotee she destroys. Both may be called the oceanic mother, of Geza Roheim.[20] These writers amass evidence in patterns that hold. All will hold, not because a universal relativism prevails in human thought, but because the stuff on which myth works is so endlessly adaptable.

It is, then, whole systems from culture to culture, and not just one or another figure or event in a single myth, that are translatable one into the other. Syncretism is possible also for another, perhaps related reason: the myths, in single details and in multiple complexes, are strikingly repeated all over the world in cultures that cannot have had any connection with one another. The thousands of items in Stith Thompson's *Motif Index of Folk Literature* are a monument to this riddling fact. But the translatability of myth and the recurrence of myth do not combine to demonstrate the primacy of some single coherent pattern; rather, they demonstrate how magnetic the patterns may be on this enchanted ground.

So the adaptability of mythic detail cannot be used to prove that history went a certain way: with Robert Graves that the Irish came from Greece via Spain, or with Dumézil that certain mythic congruences demonstrate the same social structure for ancient India and primitive Rome.[21] Nor can it show, with Lévi-Strauss, that the mind works in interlocking binary series just because myths lend themselves to that sort of reclassification.

The theoretical superiority of Lévi-Strauss to all the unitary interpreters of modern times—though he surpasses them, he does not supplant them—resides in his providing a system which preserves the complexity of the myth. He gives us not a magic integer number to solve all the equations, but rather an algebraic theory of transformation that stresses the complexity of relation among details, rather than their assimilability one to another.

His achievement persists even after we reject the claim of finality on which he asserts his method must rest, "legitimate only on condition that it is exhaustive."[22] If one gave random explanations (historical and logical in this case), he says, then "structural analysis would rest wholly on begged questions, and would lose its sole justification, which resides in its codage at once unique and most economical (of mythic messages)." But in such a relational world, no priority can be assigned to any formula or set of formulas: his explanation is not "unique," nor does it follow the scientific principle of economy any better than the explanations of others do. Its merit, in fact, resides in the value it places on the complexity of combinatory freedom; it is a fuller explanation than Frazer's or Graves', but not a more total one. All his details can be translated into Frazer's pattern as readily as Frazer's into his. He surpasses his predecessors not by being more economical, but precisely in refusing to be as economical as they themselves are.

The explanation, of course, may overwhelm the fact, the person may get obscured by his personae. In ritual this is accounted for. Ritual provides a special, perhaps seasonal, moment in which the self-obscuring of the person may be regarded as a self-transcendence. But if this moment is itself generalized, if the myth is asserted to dominate, as by Eliade,[23] and to take the individual fact out of time, the coherence of this circle leaves the breaks in the circle unaccountable, as well as the transritual discontinuities of full human life, which such an account has to deploy, but which tragedy either celebrates or at least tries to visualize in time, while out of time. We can accept the plausibility of Eliade's renewals and returns without allowing them either ultimate significance or dominance. So the adaptability of the emotions' dynamic stuff may allow Norman O. Brown to substitute Romulus and Remus coherently for Oedipus, but it does not then follow that the fits and starts, the special but vast constructions of historical fact, are then to be subjected to a cycle of myths of which the warring brothers is the logical first.[24]

The depth explanation that ignores sequence lays itself open to the fallacy that Brown does generate; in asserting the connection between an unconscious myth-pattern and the perceived item of fact, he goes further and asserts their necessary identity. Such an identification, in destroying the distinction between unconscious and conscious, between myth and fact, paradoxically renders impossible their interaction in the drama or in history itself. "All typology is eschatology,"[25] he would say, and therewith would nullify the essential condition of time, past, present, and future.

Wholly to submerge the fact in the myth is to lose the possibility of discussing their relation, and it is only in their relation to each other that either may be clearly seen. For a Greek tragedy, as for any literary work, the uniqueness of one work combines, as it must for access to emotional material, the patterns of myth. But even so complex a system of myth-structuring as Northrop Frye's, even after its internal inconsistencies and shifts in terminology are ironed out, while it succeeds in giving an order for myth comparable in complexity to Lévi-Strauss's, fails to provide the terms in which the actual combinatory complexities of a given work might be described, let alone valued. (In eschewing value, Frye feels he has obviated the necessity of dealing with the complexities of the unique work or, in effect, even of providing a method for doing so.) If his form-types overlap in a given work, or even if their omnipresence is conceivable in some full work like the *Divine Comedy*, the application of them would become truistic once its arbitrariness became clear in the examination of actual relations. It would not matter whether we referred to *agon, sparagmos, pathos,* or *anagnorisis*.[26]

3

Dionysus partakes of the sign-system of every Greek tragedy. His altar is visible in the significant space of the bare stage; a sacrifice and other ritual devotions precede the play; his priest sits in an honored labeled chair of superior marble in the first row, a chair winged significantly with griffins.[27] The intentional or conative thrust of an entire play, or a series of plays, aims at a kind of act of worship of him. That tragedy seemed at once to drift away from such an explicit act—as the ancient comment asserts, "nothing toward Dionysus,"[28]—only affirms the connection.

Dionysus is more than a sign connecting facts to myth, vines to the Vine, the whole seasonal cycle to the Vine's ripe moment in it, and the transport of the imbibing person to Vine and Season. Nor is the sign expressible by a simple formula. Sets of designata swarm under the single name Dionysus. Since both honey (in the ritual invocations of bacchants, *Bacchae*, 142-3) and ashes (the end of *Semele*) enter into the myth of Dionysus, all the interlocking sets of *Du Miel aux cendres* might be adapted, *mutatis mutandis*, from South American Indian myth to Dionysus and applied to the Greek dramatic performance. But even a general extension of his significance over that of his contrary Apollo (unsurprisingly, if the myth reconciles contraries,[29]) so that he comes to indicate "the fraternal confluence of life and death,"[30] if left by itself, will displace into a concept his essential function of arousing, behind the ordering of disparate facts, that very emotional transport out of which the contraries rise and to which, mysteriously and ulti-mately, they refer. "The duality (of life and death)" does not just "have its symbol in the mask."[31] The mask unifies over the face of a real actor not just a symbol but an evocation, the "pity and terror," those reconciled contraries rendered pure for the actor (!), as Else reads Aristotle, but certainly for the spectator too.

Myth is neutral to a particular linguistic formulation,[32] so that the Oedipus story, as an ordering of experience, may be put in a number of different verbal sequences. Myth functions as a language "on another level" in that it carries a signification, and this signification is an ordering. With the ordering, crucially and finally, comes a charge, the emotional stuff that the myth manages and evokes as it orders.

In a play the charge of the mythos is deployed freely by that of which the myth in conception is free, a set of verbal sequences, not just (1) the logos of attributive statements, but the (further) *logoi* (2) of interaction between masked persons making the statements, (3) of the significance-loaded meters into which the statements are poured, and, finally, (4) of the play's total relation, in its combined *logoi*, not only to its own mythos (Medea or Oedipus or Hippolytus) but (5) to the "other" central mythos to which reference is always somehow being made, the myth of Dionysus. First the logos slants Hippolytus, and then the slanted *Hippolytus* stands in some significative relation to the mythos which provides a context for it, to Dionysus. A late play like Euripides' *Bacchae*, and perhaps also such lost plays of Aeschylus, as *The Semele, Dionysus' Nurses, Bacchae, Xantriai, Pentheus*, and the *Lycurgos* tetralogy provide a zero case: the mythos slanted towards Dionysus is that of Dionysus himself. But even if in some possibly recoverable past we knew that the play had arisen just from dithyrambic performances about Dionysus, the *Bacchae*, in our imagined present of spectators at its performance—a single performance as Euripides framed it—would still relate freely to the mythos of the Dionysiac festival. In choosing to worship Dionysus by a play on Dionysus, whether by invention or reversion, Euripides has not identified the play with the ritual. Rather he has invoked the significative possibilities inherent in having the invented play and the given ritual converge on the same mythos, Dionysus slanted to Dionysus.

In the generality, and also in the ambivalence, of its naming, the myth escapes the rule to which language is regularly subject, of congruence between signifier and signified. The sign points at an idea of the object: "horse" designates one class of objects, a class that would include the smaller classes of "colt," "mare," "palomino," "Percheron," and the like. So, for synonyms of abstraction, "thought," "concept," "idea," "notion," "logical point," and the like. Or even the names of feeling, "fear," "anxiety," "apprehension," "dread," "fright," or the sequence of "desire," "love," etc. But, as Cassirer follows Max Müller in pointing out,[33] mythic entities regularly give many names for a single large connection of myth to fact, in "polynomy," and because the connection of myth to fact is both loose and inclusive, they also give one name to many: "synonymy." Apollo, on the evidence of Otto, may even include Dionysus.

All the abstractions named above, moreover, may be attributed to either; and so may all the emotions, the "fear" series as well as the "desire" series. "Centaur," by Lévi-Strauss's rules of transformation, may be extended at will to polynomial complexity on the axes man–animal, man–god, permissible–impermissible (Ixion begot the Centaur on the cloud he thought was Hera), male–female, chthonic–Olympian, benevolent (Chiron-Achilles)–malevolent (Nessus-Heracles), disruptive sex (Centaurs) and wedding (Lapiths), and their combinations. The bold name "Centaur" in simple synonymy, covers all these areas.

In its relation to language, the myth does not have to undergo the processes to which diction and syntax are subjected (though one may invent such for the myth) in order to transfer and combine. The language of literature, in Jakobson's formulation, avails itself of the strategies of selection (metaphor) and combination (metonymy). But it would be a metaphoric use of those very terms to call the identification and generalization by which myth transposes fact either a metaphoric one or a metonymic one. A literary work transforms its comments, one may say, not only by intensified syntactic strategies of deploying metaphor and metonymy in its intellectual operations; but also, and concurrently, by unifying its comment in the affective sphere, by evoking an emotional series if the work is viewed in its necessary temporal sequence of word after word and sentence after sentence, by getting through to the strange underlying stuff to which myth also gets through. Sometimes it does so by employing particular myths in its mythic work. It need not do so: a poem bare of all but flat statements may contain the necessary affective sequences and evocations. The function of literature in Greece is precisely to render the mythic work available, through and beyond myth. It would be superfluous, or rather anachronistic, to say that for the Greek, "literature" is "religion," when, whatever may have been the case in prehistory, the festivals and the poems and plays existed in the same modal universe, relating to one another as part to whole (a Pindaric poem was part of a whole athletic celebration, a play of Sophocles part of the whole Dionysiac festival), so that in one sense the literary work was something less than the celebration; but also, in the relation of transform (a play of Sophocles as a significative universe including the festival as part of its reference) to base (the Dionysiac festival as a given ritual) the play is something more.

Plato's myths, light as air, exhale something of a poetic fragrance, attenuated far beyond the density the mere name Dionysus carries. In their freedom of fantasy, they have something of the fixedness of philosophic terms, without being subject to the laboriousness of proof. They are a kind of linguistic shorthand.

But the myths on which Aeschylus, Sophocles, and Euripides draw are translinguistic in their significative strategies. The ideas of these playwrights derive a compelling affective strength, and not just a poetic aura, from their saturation in myths that are cultural givens. Given they must be, precisely for the playwright to operate freely, and at the same time powerfully, upon them, beyond the binary-switch-board freedom of Lévi-Strauss, or even the theological open-endedness described by Kitto.[34] The myth, brought into a dramatic picture, generalizes fact by organizing the emotion underlying the fact. That power is implacable; Dionysus cannot be diminished or turned away. But the very implacability that permits the tragic poet access to its power, and thus to an inescapable margin of piety, shuts the door against facile pious solutions or a merely automatic devotion. The very givenness of the myth demands freedom in its dramatic handling.

4

How commandingly in the context of Athens and all Greece the play-wrights reimagined the myths is shown not only by their freedom with details of the story, but also by the fact that other representations continued to follow them. Once Euripides had invented his Medea slaying her own children, the vase painters followed suit for centuries; and often either the first or the most important revision of a myth comes from the imagination of a playwright.[35]

But one freedom did not have to resemble another. Euripides re-invents his staple mythic figures from play to play, and the Helen of the *Andromache* differs from the Helen of the *Helen*, as both do from the Helen of the *Iphigenia at Aulis*, whose central figure, in turn, has been reinvented from the *Iphigenia at Tauris*. Orestes there, moreover, differs from play to play, as Menelaus does; though Euripides also remains free to repeat himself—the Menelaus of the *Trojan Women* resembles that of the *Orestes* and the *Andromache*—all three differ radically from the coping husband of the *Helen*.

Sophocles, by contrast, retains a profound harmony of persons. The "good" Odysseus of the *Ajax* may be reconciled, as in a different situation, from the "bad" Odysseus of the *Philoctetes* forty years later, and Oedipus and Creon remain the same, while their spheres are widened from play to play.

In Aeschylus, so far as one can tell from the extant plays, all persons in their mythical combinations utilize their resources so fully under stress that little room is left for the variability of differentiation. The Danaids are absorbed in envisioning death, whether their own in the threatened suicide of the *Suppliants*, or that of their prospective husbands in the following plays of the trilogy. Clytemnestra dwells totally in exultation over the murder she commits, and then in apprehension over the one she suffers. Prometheus carries a losing struggle to cosmic proportions; even Atossa, rudimentary as she is, is nothing but all ears, throughout the *Persians*, toward the success and fate of her son.

For all the playwrights, the myths are not only a timeless staple that projects an idealized temporal sequence of some model story into a realm where time cyclically transcends itself; the myth also embodies the past. Myths, when they involve persons, are at the same time legends, and the play ripens the remote past into daimon-charged form.

The remoteness may be orchestrated, as in the *Oresteia* or the *Oedipus at Colonus*, which bring the pastness into view. Or it may be muted in the presentation. In the *Ion*, a myth where Euripides exercises a double freedom, since it is an obscure if not an unprecedented story about which he freely invents details, the remote past is brought into view clearly for the end of the play: Ion is the eponymous founder of the Ionians, from whom the Athenians of the present audience are descended. But the legendary complexities are tied off. Nothing is made of Creusa's complex past, the death, sacrifice, and war of the clan of Erechtheus. Nor do Prometheus, Deucalion and Helen emerge from behind Xuthus.

Usually, of course, the complexities of the myth's model story are schematized in the presentation. In the *Andromache* (547–765), when Peleus interposes between Menelaus and the heroine, the father of the man who killed her husband presents, ironically, her only refuge; and the background between Hector and Achilles charges the confrontation, even before Peleus adduces both law and principle to contravert Menelaus's claim over Andromache's life. This is still not the main

connection, but rather an aspect of the precedent irony, that
Andromache is linked to Peleus's grandson, Neoptolemos, whose
marriage to Hermione, the daughter of Menelaus, puts her into the
further relation of rivalry and slavery to men who have their own
condensed marital stories, Menelaus with Helen and Peleus with the
divine figure Thetis. It is indeed at the altar of Thetis that Andromache
has initially taken refuge, and parental pieties are linked with divine
in her appeal:

> Surely you have heard and know about strife in the house
> Of this man's daughter, for which I am to die.
>
> And now they are trying to drag me away
> From the altar of Thetis, who gave birth
> To your well-born son, whose marvel you revere . . .
>                                                          (563–67)

Thetis here serves as the momentary focal point for the convergence
of ambivalence-charged complexities in the model human history and
the power inherent in the gods who cross them (a power single at the
moment), as though any god would do. But beyond these schematiza-
tions, both the power and the convergence remain problematical in
the play, as it ends by saying, in Euripides' theme-exodos:

> XO. πολλαὶ μορφαὶ τῶν δαιμονίων,
>     πολλὰ δ' ἀέλπτως κραίνουσι θεοί·
>     καὶ τὰ δοκηθέντ' οὐκ ἐτελέσθη,
>     τῶν δ' ἀδοκήτων πόρον εὗρε θεός.
>     τοιόνδ' ἀπέβη τόδε πρᾶγμα.
>
> Many are the forms of daimonic things,
> Much do the gods bring about by surprise.
> The expected is not achieved.
> For the unexpected the god finds a way,
> And so has this action gone.                     (1284–88)

But we expect the unexpected. Knowing the myth, we know there is
ultimately no sure refuge for Andromache. The play maximizes the

complexities of the unexpected by turning the complexities of the expected this way and that, by allowing no closed causal set for the merging of the myth-pattern and the dramatized event.

The unpredictability of interaction between myth and event persists even when the action is simplified and the figures allegorized, as in the *Prometheus*, where the tremendous assurance of the figure whose name signified Forethought encounters the tremendous counter force of the Ruler of the universe, also the tremendous doubt of his divine servants; and finally, in this first play of the trilogy, the tremendous counteraction of being not just immobilized but also buried away from the light of day. A simple lament, a simple challenge, leave the unknown unknown: Prometheus will only hint at that, and the known is plain as day. The daughters of Oceanus, in their lament, declare that the waters of ocean, and its very depths, join in:

> The surge of the sea shouts
> As it falls together; the depth groans . . .  (431–32)

Prometheus replies by saying that, though he has been responsible, he need not speak: the simplicity of his role transfixes him in a conspectus of knowing (συννοίᾳ) that rends him in feeling:

> Don't think it because of indulgence or self-will
> That I am silent. By knowing I devour my heart,
> Seeing myself maltreated in this way.
> And yet who else than I effectively
> Defined prerogatives for these new gods?     (436–40)

Having somehow handed out the forces to gods and men does not remove the Titan from subjection to them, or the Titan's spectators, in the pressure of their own unpredictabilities.

5

In the *Hippolytus* of Euripides, all is predictable, in the usual sense: we know that myth, and anyway this playwright has written an earlier *Hippolytus*. Moreover, it is predictable in a very precise sense. In the prologue of the play Aphrodite tells us generally what (we already know) will happen. She also tells us, generally, why, and thus renders the play problematic as well as predictable, because we cannot take just her version of the reason. She is counterbalanced by Artemis, who ends the play as Aphrodite begins it. Statues of both gods stand visible on the stage, to receive homage during the action.

Further doubled problematically against these doubled gods, myths in our sense, is the central myth of the play, a myth in the more restricted Greek sense of mythos, a story about a legendary figure. The play presents an *aition* or causal story about how the cult[36] of Hippolytus got started at Troezen, the little community by a stretch of sand across the gulf from Athens. The tragedy somehow issues in success, the cult figure exists permanently as a resource for the Hellenes, and as a consolation, so to speak, for himself—a point Artemis makes at the end. Aphrodite's inexplicable torments play themselves out in a strange sentiment of forgiveness, much as the combustion of Semele, mentioned in the play (559), may result in the "double birth" (διγόνοιο, 560) of that god Dionysus, whom this play must, among other acts, be worshiping, and who, again, is mentioned in the play as the husband of Phaedra's sister Ariadne (Διονύσου δάμαρ, 339).

Aphrodite has the first word, as well as the decisive control over events, and she speaks of her power before she recounts its effects, beginning with a word which emphasizes, in its common meaning, her diversity, though it may also imply her force,[37] πολλή many:

> ΑΦ. Πολλὴ μὲν ἐν βροτοῖσι κοὐκ ἀνώνυμος
> θεὰ κέκλημαι Κύπρις οὐρανοῦ τ᾿ ἔσω.
> ὅσοι τε πόντου τερμόνων τ᾿ Ἀτλαντικῶν
> ναίουσιν εἴσω φῶς ὁρῶντες ἡλίου,
> τοὺς μὲν σέβοντας τἀμὰ πρεσβεύω κράτη·
> σφάλλω δ᾿ ὅσοι φρονοῦσιν εἰς ἡμᾶς μέγα.
> ἔνεστι γὰρ δὴ κἀν θεῶν γένει τόδε,
> τιμώμενι χαίρουσιν ἀνθρώπων ὕπο.
> δείξω δὲ μύθων τῶνδ᾿ ἀλήθειαν τάχα·

Much among mortals and not without a name,
I am called the goddess Kypris, and in heaven:
As many as between Pontus and the Atlantic bounds
Are dwelling and behold the light of the sun
And reverence me, to them I accord my powers;
But I deceive whoever think big against us.
For there is this in the nature of the gods:
They are delighted when they are honoured by men.
I shall demonstrate the truth of these myths very soon.

                                                                          (1–9)

Giving her powers is governed by an interactive law whose truth the play will demonstrate.

Everyone knows this law, about the gods and about Aphrodite in particular. Even Hippolytus does, negatively. The chorus echoes wonder in their expressions of fear. Nor must we characterize[38] the nurse as a cynical old figure sharing the homely relativism of her counterparts in *Romeo and Juliet* and *Othello*. Behind her mask, like everyone, she subjects individuation to the main thrust of expounding recititatively and exemplifying. When she says,

            Why talk so high?
    Your need is not for words well-schematized
    But for the man,                            (490–91)

she exactly echoes a Freudian principle that rationalization remains restless until desire is satisfied.

Since she is in the mythos, she cannot know its outcome. Without that knowledge, she must plead her assumption, one that the play demonstrates to be correct. There is, of course, as the play also demonstrates, a realm of counterassumption, where the logos of shame, chastity, fidelity, and family cohesiveness shades into the mythos of Artemis. But the nurse is no more responsible for that counter-assumption than she can be, nor would it help her advice if she summarized the two. A choice must be made, and under stress she recommends a choice which, in her terms, cannot be refuted; it can only enter the play as one half of a problem for which she is the persuasive spokesman, as well as the wise witness.

Aphrodite does preponderate. Her power to overturn the proud is
linked with her power over universal generation (441–66), a point
made by the nurse, and the plot bears it out; but the chorus echoes it,
singing an Aphrodite hymn (1268–81) at the inappropriate moment
after Hippolytus's death. At the same time, beyond the staged events
Artemis gets strengthened; the result of the plot is that the cult of
Hippolytus is founded, and Artemis sees to that. Aphrodite has not
only the first word, but the force; Artemis has the last word, but only
a concessive reconciliation.

Yet the cult of Hippolytus is a marriage cult! And the precincts of
both his temples, at Troezen and at Athens, contained a shrine to
Aphrodite.[39] And not only in Greek legend, but within the play,
Artemis shades somewhat ambivalently into her opposite, in her form
as Dictynna (146, 1130) a figure from Phaedra's place of origin, Crete.
The bee of Artemis (77), as Knox points out,[40] is transferred to
Aphrodite (562–63).

Knox goes on to point out that this doubling of one by the other
reaches its climax at the end when Artemis "repeats word after word
and phrase after phrase of Aphrodite's prologue."[41]

But Artemis is having her say. Mainly the spheres are kept apart;
Aphrodite is given the beginning and Artemis the end. Since both
operate, connections can shade into confusions. Both statues are visible
on the stage, as some kind of parallel to the altar of Dionysus visible
before it. The chorus (713) swears by Artemis to keep silent about the
action of Aphrodite.

The focus remains on Aphrodite. In her last speech (724–31),
Phaedra complains about how she "delights" Aphrodite for "destroying
her" when she has been "worsted by a bitter love." Yet she declares,
finally, that she will punish Hippolytus for taking an attitude of pru-
dence ($\sigma\omega\phi\rho\sigma\nu\epsilon\hat{\iota}\nu$, 731) that can only derive from a distrust of Aphrodite
similar to the very one she is voicing. He stays with this attitude,
declaring, as though it would save him, that no man is more prudent
than he ($\sigma\omega\phi\rho\sigma\nu\acute{\epsilon}\sigma\tau\epsilon\rho\sigma\nu$, 1100) as he goes off to an imagined exile, but
actually to death with an apotheosis, attributable to him from the
context of his shrine in the lives of the spectators.

Coming hard upon the chorus's "inappropriate" last hymn to
Aphrodite (1268–81), and echoing somewhat their excited dochmiacs,
the epiphany of Artemis instantly transposes the concerns of the play,

and the feelings too. Restoration and resolution take over from questions of health, justice, and domination. "You alone rule" (μόνα κρατύνεις, 1281), were the chorus's last words, but Artemis replaces power by a rational assessment:

> Did you kill your son impiously?
> Believing the invisible in your wife's
> False tales? You hold visible madness. (1287–89)

She keeps insisting that she does not intrude on the domain of Aphrodite and she does not judge between the "goad" (οἶστρον, 1300) and the "nobility" (γενναιότητα, 1301) of Phaedra, merely providing the kind of assertions proper to her own domain. Even for one who has done dread things (δείν᾽ ἔπραξας, 1325) there is pardon. This has already operated for Theseus, and his injustice has been resolved before the expiring Hippolytus enters to prove his own need of resolution by calling the father "unjust" (1348). Artemis stands calmly ready to dissolve the dramatic irony of this ignorance, though she does not speak until he has given the full vent of fifty choral lines to his misery and pain. Since he calls out to Zeus and to the chorus, but not to his "dearest of gods" (as she says, 1394), he must be presumed to be held in a present irony as well as a past; he does not see Artemis on stage. Their stichomythy plays on the ambivalence of tenderness and implacability in her attitude (a version of the delight contradicting terror in Aphrodite). Once Artemis has lined up father and son—and Phaedra—into equivalence as victims of Aphrodite (1404), Theseus can join his resolution to his son's in mutual forgiveness, but not in the curse against Aphrodite that Artemis immediately arrests (1416 ff.). To balance their ills (ἀντὶ τῶνδε τῶν κακῶν, 1423), she describes the "highest honors" (τιμὰς μεγίστας, 1424) of the cult she is founding for him. He will be "not nameless" (1429), a term that has been applied to both Artemis and Aphrodite in the play. These are her last words, and she departs to let him die without her, because "it is not ordained for me to look at corpses" (ἐμοὶ γὰρ οὐ θέμις φθιτοὺς ὁρᾶν, 1437), supreme implacability following upon supreme tenderness. Playing out the mutual appeal of shared sorrow, he dies as the hero-father urges his son to "hold out" (καρτέρει, 1456), and declares, in his last words, that he will remember the "multitude of evils" ascribable to Kypris.

The suffering again was "unexpected," as the last chorus says in its refrain (ἀέλπτως, 1463). That the great are suffering only makes the suffering greater (1465–66), the last words reminding the audience of the magnification that the mythic material has performed upon the terrestrial commonplace of conflicting forces and destructive powers.

Aphrodite and Artemis do not stand in strict antinomy here; they supersede and outflank each other. Nor are they the only gods present, since Theseus is able to kill his son through the agency of a third, Poseidon, a god whom in the play he calls his father. Fatherhood is given as the reason for the curse: it is thus by being a son that he can eliminate a son. (And earlier [794] he had presumed, on arriving to the alarm of the chorus, that something had happened, not to his wife, but to his mortal father, Pittheus.)

Poseidon does not appear in his own form, but in that of a bull materializing by the sea, an animal that may[42] signify sexuality like any large animal, but who stands as an icon of much more general mythic forces even than sexuality, as Poseidon himself does. Those forces, moreover, are associated locally (though not in the language of the play) with the place of Phaedra's origin, Crete. The only other occurrence of the word in the play refers to the "love for the bull held" (ἔρον, . . . ὃν ἔσχε ταύρου, 337–38) by Phaedra's mother, Pasiphae.

This returns us to Aphrodite's domination over the complex past of these legendary families. Phaedra refers to her own descent, the infatuations of her mother and her sister Ariadne,[43] but Theseus is silent about his abandonment of Ariadne, as about his conquest of the Amazon ("breastless") mother of Hippolytus; and only if we extend his last curse of Kypris into an indefinite future can he be conceived of as deflecting his prior subjection to Aphrodite. Even in the world of familial prudence a problem is created by the contrast between the illegitimacy of Hippolytus and the legitimacy of Phaedra's children. Here are several Freudian patterns: Hippolytus's narcissistically tinged chastity as a resentment for his father's undervaluation of the Amazon; Phaedra's passion as a compulsive act of revenge against her husband's absence and infidelity; Hippolytus's hunting as an imitation of his father's heroism; Phaedra's legalistic incest as the only form in which she dares to imitate her mother by breaking sexual taboos. Emphasis on such patterns would only spell out the wilderness of connections generated by the paramount principle of Aphrodite's dominance.

Here, then, the *muthoi* provide not even a system of checks and balances, but a clear and mysterious urgency dominating all the *logoi* that can be mustered, including the careful pattern of abstractions that the play builds: sickness, modesty-shame-respect, thought, opinion, prudence, good report (νόσος, αἰδώς, φρονεῖν, δόξα, σωφροσύνη, εὐκλεῖα). And above these abstractions, employing them, there are many striking maxims in the play whose power echoed through the streets, to be recognizable on mere hearing more than twenty years later in the *Frogs* of Aristophanes—but not to withstand the magic binding the mythical spheres to the mythical events:

> It is necessary for gods to be wiser than mortals    (120)

In a sense this remark belies itself by at least equaling what a god might think about the question:

> We will effectuate noble things from these shames    (331)

> Kypris were not a god,
> But whatever there may be greater than a god    (359-60)

>     There are many pleasures of life,
> Long conversations, and leisure, an evil joy,
> And *modesty*.    (383-85)

The notion that modesty is a pleasure has long bothered commentators.[44]

> Believe me, for that is a delight of second rank    (508)

Nobody really understands this; or what the first rank would be.

> The tongue has sworn, but the mind has not sworn    (612)

It does not matter who is adducing these maxims, or how apt the psychology may be, since what is happening sweeps up the insufficient *logoi* of the speakers in the "tales worthy of grief" (ἀξιοπενθεῖς φῆμαι, 1465-66) of the foreknown events.

The nurse's careful psychological understanding cannot control the uncontrollable:

> Much living has taught me much.
> Mortals should stir up measured
> Loves for one another
> And not to the marrow-pitch of the soul,
> But the mind's desires should be easily loosed,
> Pushed off, and drawn together.
> It is hard and deep for one
> Soul to have birthpangs for two, as I
> Suffer in excess for her.                          (252–60)

Care, in the power of Aphrodite, is itself easily loosed.

Beyond this lies not just the concluding, ambivalent tenderness of Artemis and the cult whose other shrine was a stone's throw from the theater, but a vision of peaceful delights, "sublimated" as we would say, in the nature where blossom the meadows spoken of early by both Hippolytus (74) and Phaedra (211). He evokes the same tonality of tenderness when he recalls in foreseen retrospection, at the moment of exile, the blessings of a young life in Troezen:

> How many blessings you have in which to live one's youth!
>                                                          (1096)

This qualifying tonality, which is attributable neither to Artemis nor to Aphrodite but shares something of both, dominates all four long choruses, in the relative calm of Aeolic measures, and also in the relative excitement of dochmiacs at moments of stress.

The chorus enters invoking the waters of Oceanus dripping from a rock (123) to ask about a possible cure for their mistress. Their ensuing stasimon, which lists the victims of Eros, still ends with the fluttering honeybee (563). When they desire, after Phaedra's suicide speech, to fly away like a bird, it is toward the islands of the Hesperides where grow the apples that are the wedding gifts of Hera:

> where the holy-blessing earth
> grows happiness for the gods                  (750–51)

At the exile of Hippolytus, finally, they mourn the instability of human life (1102–41) but conclude by a reference to the Graces (1148).

This "pastoral" vision—to wrench the label of another genre—does not modify the tragic one, or do more than give a kind of imaginative extension, in the poetic *logoi*, to the poignancy of Artemis at the end. Beyond these tonalities is the monotone severity of the central event, the death of a young man merely because of erotic spite on the one hand and chaste silence on the other (Sophocles' *Phaedra* presumably made the woman a protagonist, a shift that would have to have provided quite different transformations on the same base).

Within the play, too, and throughout, the silences and the utterances counteract one another, as Bernard Knox points out.[45] Managed silences, and their violation, provide the main dramatic progression of the play. Heavy taboos bind the words; they charge as a special device, to the second degree as it were, what is present to the first degree in all plays: an interchange of words about some things, a lack of interchange about others.

Both come together here under the taboos. The myths charge the taboos.

And the play charges the myths; its *logoi* within, transcended by the *mythoi*, themselves contain the transcendence: Aphrodite stands beyond the shame-respect-prudence cluster, but by contradicting the Artemis who also stands beyond them by the poignant tenderness she somehow makes prevail, lingering over her Olympian withdrawal.

6

When Plato[46] burned his tragedies, he was turning away, and turning toward. Philosophy was to do it better, say it truer. In our *panoptikon* of time, we may stand and look between his turns, tragedy this way, philosophy that. We incorporate the past, this way and that, catching it all up in between. The Aristotle, Vernant[47] recaptures, could not recapture tragedy. Straining, we recapture the philosophy, the logos, at the heart of tragedy, the mythos. From mythos to logos, Nestle[48] says, but logos resides in mythos. Greek tragedy remarkably fuses the myth and the verbalized thought.

Plato, nursed on tragedy, brought mythos and logos together: his own *mythoi* are versions of his *logoi*. "So I have spoken both a mythos and a logos," he has one say.[49] And Socrates says of his final myth in the *Gorgias*, "What you, I believe, consider *mythos*, I consider *logos*."[50] In this light, words have a certain urgency, "I am bitten by the *logoi* in philosophy," says Alcibiades, "which have a bite more savage than a viper."[51] He says it in a dialogue about love, linking love and thought.

Enactment recasts the recitation of dithyramb or *epinikion* into a form where the actors, somewhat raised on their cothurni, boom out from behind their donned masks the words that are spaced and rhythmed round an explanation of a known myth. The drama, angling the myth toward its explanation, patterns it in an affective sequence that forms the explanation into a contour of the silent spectator's time. The interchange of normal speech is suppressed; hearing what transpires on the stage, the spectator instead of speaking up, doubles back in his silence and sees out there, in the mythical others who are blessed with this heightened measuring of words, what is the unknown in his actual world, the secret link between the thought that the words express and the Dionysian ritual out of which the play is enacted. In the bright sunlight logos and mythos take each other over. Each play, given once for all time, concentrates its urgency into an obbligato of freedom for the given, doubling a unique performance over a set of liturgy; a special, invented form over the given myth. This doubling becomes single, renewing the unknown in the myth as explained, or given the explanation of not being explained. Euripides' signature is the reassurance of explanation amid the polymorphousness of the daimonic:[52]

> Many are the forms of daimonic things,
> Much do the gods bring about by surprise.
> The expected is not achieved.
> For the unexpected the god finds a way,
> And so has this action gone.

And Sophocles has his chorus of old men, who have lived to the point where they can forget the passions (as Plato says of this playwright in *The Republic*[53]), close in a notion new for the play by asking the Thebans—all the Greeks in the audience who are supposed not to overhear—

> behold this Oedipus
> Who solved the famous riddle, was your mightiest man.
> What citizen on his lot did not with envy gaze?
> See to how great a surge of dread fate he has come!
> (1524–27)

These reassurances come at the end of dire events; or rather, at the
enactment of dire events, wherein we get one kind of doubling, setting
a story both past in the racial history and permanent in the god-
managing ritual out there before the eyes, on a special day. This one
kind of doubling has done duty for the other, the unknown purpose of
life toward which all religions refer. In this we might participate as
ritual purifiers, or haunted murderers, or even theorizing speakers.
Mythos and logos come together because, they have been doubled in
and through the stage action. We stand aside (as the idealized Greek
spectators we become when we contemplate Greek tragedy).


We resemble the Greeks in a second sense: not only in a willingness to
resemble them by attending to their *mythoi* and *logoi*, but also in finding
mythos as problematic to logos. Our time, beginning with the Industrial
Revolution, doubles back on its own consciousness and discovers,
through Blake and hosts of others, that mere logos will not render our
sense of our lives, we need mythos. Logical thought, the Cartesian or
the Wittgensteinian, we can take for granted, but the myth asks the
dire Blakean or Freudian questions. The Greeks, while they could take
myth for granted, found the dire questions in logical thought. For them,
as for us, mythos was in tension with logos, though logos pulled at them
as mythos pulls at us.

In our *panoptikon* of time, all times are brought to life, man as the
measure of all things, reduced from the Christian mystery but not
canceled from it; the Greece, the inner Greece, becomes enacted in
Aeschylus, Sophocles, and Euripides. We recover the tragic light, and
the tragic body, that account for the long shadow of mythos over logos
through Plato into the Neoplatonists. The mythos, held in the doubling
view of tragedy, yields significations as well as enigmas. As Maximus
of Tyre said, "*Mythoi* are less apparent than the *logos* but clearer than
a riddle."[54]

# Chapter Two: THEATRON

## 1

A Greek theatrical spectacle manages the loaded silence of its spectators by a unified act of participatory speech, one both unique and universal. Once a play was given, it could not be given again, and it was given to a Panhellenic audience, the whole world of its time. The terms for the performance bring it into rapport with other activities too. *Theatron* signifies the "house" of live spectators as well as the place where they watched, and the root of the word spreads over a much larger participatory world than that of the theater: *theoros*, "beholder," with its abstract counterpart *theoria*, signifies someone consulting an oracle or taking part in a festival, a spectator at public games as well as at the theater, and also an official overseer in certain states.

In the single Greek theatrical performance, the *legomena* of a play converge with the *dromena* of a rite. Elements often separated in society, such as speculative discourse and devotional worship—elements pressing for separation in the Greek society where tragedy came into being—were bound together in the words, meters, and music of the dramatic performance. It unites and transposes such verbal sources as simple Dionysiac dithyramb, "iambic" poem, and epic mythos. As Nietzche says[1] "The drama is complete with a new vision . . . . The Dionysiac chorus . . . keeps emptying itself into a world of Apollonian images . . . . Each part of the chorus, with which tragedy is woven through, is at the same time the matrix of the whole so-called dialogue, that is, of the entire state world, the real drama. The drama renders into Apollonian sensibility the Dionysiac conceptions and effects, and by this means it is sundered from the epic as by a monstrous abyss."

The mythos, Dionysian or Apollonian or their fusion, picks up *logoi*; thereby the generality of an emotion (mythos) is bodied forth "out there on stage" in the analyzable particularity of a fact, something happening through specific words. Fixed on one side of the speech act as a permanent addressee, the spectator is split into an abstract silence.

This limit revises the normal conflation of emotion and thought by putting the spectator (whose perception receives the meaning of the play) in a position where he has accessible to him only a silent emotion (so that he cannot verbalize his thought; he can only act as a sounding board). Correspondingly, the play in the classic Greek theater seizes the possibility of redressing that overbalance of emotion by heightening the thought-component in the notably abstract language of the dialogue; then by restructuring it around musical interludes that are closer to the ritual origins (Dionysiac dithyrambs) than the dialogue is. This whole enactment is all brought to bear on the *mythoi*, orderings of that very emotion which is the silent spectator's sole resource.

The split his silence imposes on the spectator involves him in an exacting relation to the language of the play. As André Green says "The contradiction the spectator undergoes is such that while the *project* of being at the theater initially brought about a split between the theater and the world, the *fact* of being at the spectacle replaces the confrontation between the space of the theater and that of the world (now become invisible . . .) by that between the theatrical space which is visible and the theatrical space which is invisible."[2] However defined, the spectator's new relation gives him an absolute freedom to see something "unconnected" with his past, in the absolute limit of staying silent in his seat. At his known, stationary point of vision, he will open his eyes on the unknown. The fixity of his limit provides a psychological fulcrum for entering with mind and heart into the coherence of what a transcendence of limits will posit and enact.


The stage exists in, and reflects, a total social context, as do other societal formulations, even one so seemingly direct as a gift.[3]

To discuss, then, the relation of the actual stage to the larger actual group gathering it, and of the actual stage to the imagined scenes upon it, we must determine the larger context of the stage. And determining its context also determines that of the linguistic act that its statements constitute. For a simple linguistic act, we could tell by intonation, probably, whether a woman was saying "Shut the door," to husband, friend, child, maid, father, employer, or priest.[4] In the more complex total linguistic act of a verbal statement set in dramatic form, we have, in addition to audible intonations, a host of visible clues and semantic situations that begin with the social context of the presentation. A Greek play is performed on specified days at a festival honoring the God Dionysus, whose altar is visibly present beside the stage. The context of a play on this stage, too, differs from the situation of an Elizabethan play, put on in a converted hotel outside the city limits because performances are hedged in by law.

The actual stage serves to connect the imagined scene of a performance with the actual scene of life. The circumstance of dramatic dialogue thus provides a fourfold set of combinations: among stage group, their imagined scene, the audience group, and their actual scene. This may be seen in a diagram:

```
                                 S
                                 T
                                 A
                                 G
                                 E

  I                           │  A
  M        S                  B  U
  A        T                  O  D      (Door
  G        A                  U  I        of
  I        G                  N  E      Theater)
  N        E                  D  N
  E                           A  C                 A
  D        G                  R  E                 C
           R                  Y                    T
  S        O                     G                 U
  C        U                     R                 A
  E        P                     O                 L
  N                              U
  E       (1)                    P                 S
 (2)                          (3)                  C
                                                   E
                                                   N
                                                   E
                                                  (4)
```

Here are diagrammed four sets of signifier-signified relationships in the semantic structure of any staged presentation: not only the main reference *(a)* from imagined scene (2) to actual scene (4), but also those between *(b)* stage group (1) and imagined scene (2), between *(c)* stage group (1) and audience group (3), and between *(d)* audience group (3) and actual scene (4).

There exist, consequently, various possibilities for points of contact between one of these terms and another. The point of contact signifies something; it means something for the *Bacchae* and the *Thesmophoriazusae* that an imagined scene involving rites takes place on an actual stage that had been, and was still to some extent at the time of the play, a scene for actual rites. The second shrine to Hippolytus stood under the Acropolis, a stone's throw from those watching that play. The imagined scene may analogize part of an actual scene, or all of it. "All the world's a stage" draws a metatheatrical full circle on this process, but the conjunction between imagined scene and actual scene admits of many modalities.

In the *Rhesus* of Euripides the eeriness of the events is set in the disparity between the sunlit stage scene and the imagined night of the military exploit, to which the actors and the chorus repeatedly refer (223, 331, 447, 528–38, 564 ff., 737, 985). In the *Choephoroi*, when Orestes addresses the sun (994 ff.), there is an actual sun overhead, and the bareness of the orchestra's imagined scene, the thin line between the stage group and the audience group to whom he is reciting, leaves the actual scene free for such references without elaborate sleights. Here, all four sets of stage-spectator relationships (*a*) through (*d*) draw closer together because we are at an actual festival which the imagined scene is part of. Somewhat earlier Orestes had referred to a darkness (661) which was imaginary but general: it embraced the whole stage, but only because he said so; his saying simplified the connection between the spoken darkness and the real darkness the audience could not see till long after the blazing daylight of the festival performance. Later, when he speaks of the Gorgons (1048), it is stated explicitly that he sees them but the chorus does not (1061). These imaginary beings do not embrace the whole stage, though they will do so in the opening of the next play of the trilogy, to which they give the title. In the *Eumenides*, the imagined scene can shift, almost without comment, from Delphi, where we are not, to Athens, where in fact we are, a stone's throw again from the Areopagus where the judgment takes place. And now the audience group (3) as potential jurors, suddenly takes on a different modality toward the imagined scene (2) because it refers so directly to a function they perform in their actual scene (4). But not for (1), the legendary and divine beings of the stage group. The elisions among these various identifications permit a simple syntax of movement from one to another.

The very profusion of possibilities for the imagined scene should put us on our guard against translating it too readily, or too totally, into an actual one. Much of Shakespeare's comedy is "festive," in Barber's phrase, and yet a delicate balance in *Twelfth Night* or *Midsummer Night's Dream* is overthrown when the connection of the imagined scene with the actual scene of seasonal ritual is drawn, however subtly, to the exclusion of the other actual scenes that are combined in the references of those plays. In a Greek play, the festival (the actual scene and the audience group) relates to the imagined scene as whole to part, and as *dromenon* to *legomenon*; the actuality of the festival rules out analogy (*a*) between imagined scene and actual scene as a significative reminiscence, but not as a partial statement, via that between stage group and actual scene (one of the further relations to which no letter was given above).


Ultimately, as a result of throwing the radical interchange in spoken language onto some separate plane of scene and stage for emphasis, a dramatic performance intensifies all its speaker-auditor relations. The actors are intensified by being separated from the spectators, whose perceptions are intensified by having them polarized apart from the actors. The separate plane, in turn, sets up an imagined scene as distinct from the actual one (to which it must refer if it is to be meaningful). The distinction intensifies each by sensitizing it to the other, by rendering its relation to the other problematical.

If it is not somehow problematical, the relation between actual and imagined scene does not allow for literature, and it is the stubborn freedom of its questioning that gives literature a special, transcendental linguistic function, apart from any aestheticism. A ritual procession which makes no distinction whatever between its actual scene and an imagined one possesses no leverage to make a comment *by itself* on any actual scene, including its own, though it may derive from a set of religious comments. That is, even the Mass, dramatic in the sense that it is performed, makes no religious comments, though its language embodies a full set of theological relationships. It gets these from the

Church but in no way reorganizes their significance. It acts, it does not comment by action.

A drama, by contrast, has the means to interrelate and develop fully, as a comment, all the elements possible for its intensification: single actors, groups of actors (choruses, etc.), a visible stage, an imagined scene, a group of spectators, a series of actions, and a series of statements. The *dromenon* itself, in such a combination, becomes also a *legomenon*.

Dramatic speech heightens a speaker's expressiveness, by building his utterance into the interactions of an imagined role in an imagined scene. To take Jakobson's set of components for the speech act, five of the emphases possible to language receive charged effects in dramatic speech; and, in dramatic verse, the sixth as well. "Emotive" language that centers on an "addresser" comes into special play in drama, because the addresser is present and visible, at least imaginably. He necessarily expresses his feelings when he speaks, by objectifying them on the magnified context of the stage, real or imagined. The conative language that tries to act on an "addressee" is also present in a drama, and doubly, since the dramatic setting structures the aim of its speeches towards two targets, an audience real or imagined, and the other actors on stage. In a dramatic monologue, of course, the "other actor" is the self; on a stage, the language must be pretending to act conatively on one's self as the addressee if no other is present then or ever.

We are always made especially aware as auditors of the context, of the referential aspect of language in dramatic speech, because the context is set formally before the eyes of body or mind, and everything said refers just to that scene, creating by each artificed expression a running reference to the artificial scene. And dramatic language also becomes doubly "phatic," occupied as it is with the contact between speaker and auditor. Only thus can it produce a special implied thrust, to get across the stage to the audience and to get through to another actor standing there formally.

All these conditions in themselves make the language on stage of its very nature "metalingual," or concerned with its "code." In the "metatheatrical" context of a stage, both the make-believe involved in having an imagined scene, and the associativeness to reality implied in the necessary relation between the imagined scene and some actual one, bring into the foreground for its speeches the code into which it has been constructed. Moreover, if the language is verse, it is also ostentatious: it calls attention to itself and to its special rhythmic and rhetorical effects, to its form as well as to its content; it is poetic.

All these intensifications emerge unified from the mouth of a single speaker. The functional intensity of his speeches heightens the actor's person into unity; and so the dramatic speech as a whole renders problematic what will be the unity of the other persons whom he calls upon to interact with him. In Greek drama the mask formalizes this unity and visibly subordinates other elements to its amplifying board.

2

The logos of the play, thus intensified in its interactive form across the stage barrier, operates on the mythos, much as language, in Lacan's formulation, restructures the Freudian internal myth-dynamics of emotion into the logical patterns of dialogue and dialectic. For Lacan,[5] all human intercourse, the unconscious and the conscious, finds its fundamental structure in the form of linguistic transaction, of dialogue, a situation that a play formalizes and a Greek play abstracts by basing itself on a rehandling of given myth. In a psychoanalysis the analyst becomes the Other with both a capital and a small O and so allows the self to become aware of itself, the Capital through the small s, by directing its dialogue with itself back to the Self, just because the Other, the analyst, remains silent. The operating analyst is passive; he merely helps the patient bridge the gaps of his hesitations and distortions in his dialogue with himself. This suppression of normal dialogue allows the patient to enter a new, transcendental dialogue, not just of intellectual apprehension, but one of a total Husserlian intentionality. The suppressed-other of the dialogue, by becoming omnipotent, makes emotion both omnipotent and manageable. The Husserlian intentionality has been put on an emotional footing, and language itself comes into its fullness as an emotional calculus. Here Lacan stands beyond Husserl, while incorporating his lessons.[6]

Now Lacan's analytic model provides a structure that gets inverted in a dramatic performance. There, too, a dialogue takes place, to which not the Other, but the self, is in a formal, abrogated silence. The condition of not speaking in this dialogue is compensated for on a stage where a kind of monologue takes place—a monologue that always follows formal rules which are not just those of ordinary language and which in most, though not all, conventions, involve verse. The monologue is itself a dialogue to the second degree: people speak to each other on stage. And in Greek drama we have two kinds of dialogue to the second degree: that between one or more of the three actors, and that spoken by the collective chorus, who may be surrogates for just one of the persons or for the playwright, as well as agents in their own right. In addition, since by origin their context of syntactic assertion makes them almost certainly in some way members of the religious procession from which the audience has been, so to speak, split off, they are surrogates for the audience in a mode different from the actors. The dialogue of the dramatic transaction, then, takes place by suppressing the speech of the self, by displacing it not just into an objective dialogue, but into two kinds of interacting dialogue. Of this abnormal dialogue the mask is not only the symbol but also the semantic vehicle. The audience, as it subjects itself to the sequence of the structured statements in the play, reacts cathartically both by identification (in so far as it is addressed), empathizing in pity; and by disidentification, in so far as its own speech is suppressed, by aroused fright, by *phobos*, in Aristotle's term. The word *phobos* occurs as a verb in key interchanges of the *Ajax*, to settle on a specific play for illustration. His *phobos* is bound to a set of signifiers, to what happens on stage in action or word. That must act for him to react, and Aristotle's term, *phobos*, in Plato's definition,[7] is precisely a reaction to a present condition, as distinct from *deos*, an apprehension of the future. But *phobos* is the intensive term that may include the other, and the reaction implies a foreboding until the drama has ended and the stage has cleared, as Bruno Snell emphasizes in building the whole transactional psychology of the dramatic performance into that one word.[8]

The initial context of this suppressed dialogue, the semantic field within which the play occurs, may itself broaden considerably the initial fact of the play, both synchronically and diachronically. A play by Sophocles about the Trojan War (and well over 30 per cent of his plays took their subjects from it[9]) organizes certain semantic choices out of the total body of permanent myth (gods and heroes) and hypostatized past (the Trojan war as the ideal form of Panhellenic action) both synchronically and diachronically. All these may converge in a central figure like Ajax, a local cult hero from nearby Salamis who refers to the Athens of the play, and whose statue is synchronically present in the Athens of the morning of the play at a prominent corner of the city. Diachronically he is a legendary hero, a person, who intersects with legendary events. The context of Sophocles' play vivifies all these religious associations by verbalizing them in the context of worship; it also makes literary references to the ideal Panhellenic poems, those of Homer, and also to the Ajax trilogy of Aeschylus and perhaps others. Aristotle refers to *Aiantes* as a type. "Religious" and "literary," both diachronically and synchronically, stand in a special kind of systemic relation in Greek society, a relation hard to parallel in other societies. This is so, even without the synchronic, and performatively crucial, condition of context, that the play is a compulsory item in a great festival to Dionysus where all the Greeks flocked in March when the seas were once again open.

In the last half of *Ajax* the imagined scene is the seashore, with nothing to be seen on the visible stage: the seashore is pure (and designatively purified) thought.

The two terms on the audience side, the viewers sitting there, and the actual scene to which they return when the play is over, do not correspond to one another: a ritual viewer at the Greater Dionysia has assumed a role which is only a part, and that a displaced part, of his role in the actual scene of "the rest" of Greek life.

In the *Ajax* we are subjected to a movement paced through the verbal contemplation of something about to happen that the audience already knows, the death of Ajax. This contemplation, as the main drift of the play, abrogates the pseudo-Aristotelian question of a disunity[10] in the play consequent upon the protagonist's early death. We are inspecting and reacting to the circumstances of his foreknown death. In the circumstances of inspection, in the narrower context of the play, there are several syntactic conditions, literary and religious surrounding the central one, that Ajax has been maddened by Athene for having twice boasted of his human self-sufficiency. The loss of the arms, which has already taken place, merely serves as the occasion for his god-given sickness, his *theia nosos,* and then for the death from which he has to be

restored first, in the play, to proper burial against the wishes of the
Greek commanders, and then, by implication, to his full status as an
Athenian cult figure. Here are some of the syntactic conditions, then,
in which we inspect the death of Ajax:

1)
   Natural
   Forces
   (as 650–75)          Men (free slave)
               Gods                  Beasts

2)
   Trojan War             Past
            Athens           Present

3)
   Family              Enemy
         State             Friend

4)
   Cult Hero
        Suffering mass

5)
   Local            Salamis
      Panhellenic        Athens
                      Troy

6)
   Sickness
        Health

7)
   *Known* in cycle
        'Unknown'—'dramatic ironies'
        and the two times

To say "known and unknown" gives us the special dynamic of the
myth in relation to the audience. That the audience knew the myth
before the play was put on is not an incidental fact. It defines the whole
progress of the action. It puts the audience at one remove, just as the
ritual arguably brings the audience closer. There is no simple suspense
about the unknown at all. Everyone knows Ajax commits suicide.
Dramatic irony, consequently, is not a special effect in this theater,
though it may surface at any time into momentary prominence. It is
a general condition of the play, which has actors who pretend not to
know what is happening put on an action that the audience already
knows. Those who may speak cannot know, and those who know

cannot speak. Even a prophet like Calchas has to peer into the future.
In the dimension of prophesying that Ajax must bear his madness for
a full day, we hear recited—we already knew—why Athene has
visited the madness upon him in the first place. In the middle of the
play, in his central speech, Ajax describes time as cyclic. The chorus,
in their joy, speak of the unhoped-for and unexpected (ἀέλπτων, 714)
that Ajax not only γιγνώσκει, "knows"—he has used the vocabulary
of knowing and seeing throughout—but μετανεγνώσθη (715), changed
his knowing of, or became converted to. Both prefixes, the *meta* and the
*ana*, insist on the change.

To life, the chorus supposes. But he has used ἄελπτον surrounded by
negatives at the beginning (648) of his speech, to which they respond.
The irony gets resolved only when the actors' circle of unknowing
closes at the point of the audience's knowing. Their last, brief chorus
declares as much:

> There is much for mortals who see
> To know. Before he sees no one is a prophet
> Of the future, how he will fare.                    (1418–20)

The grouping of the actors displays this double subjection to foreknowledge and expectation. If one looks ahead, as the *prologos* and the
*parodos* do, then the first episode looks both ahead and back, and the
others likewise. The groupings follow suit throughout the play.

The additions and subtractions to these formal groupings of no more
than three actors, and always two participants (actors and chorus), are
patterned around expectations, retrospections, and confrontations that
themselves hinge on a doubling of the known and the unknown. At
the same time, the progress of these smaller groupings moves in a
linear and ascending series to the shock of the suicide, known and
unknown, the greater shock of the refusals to bury, known and unknown, and the resolving, still greater shock of Odysseus's magnani-
mity—a new element in Sophocles' handling, and an unexpected
(ἄελπτον) aspect of the Odysseus type. Here audience and stage group
have almost come together vis-à-vis the unknown.

Back at the center, in the imagined expansion of *Ajax*, his rhetoric
encompasses our dramatic irony. Knowing he is to die, we see him

become aware of this in a kind of *anagnorisis* and conceal it from those whose joy kindles in us a horror of listening—like their shuddering.

"I shuddered with Eros" (ἔφριξ' ἔρωτι, 693), says the Chorus, as it "soars" (ἀνεπτόμαν, 693) away from this declaration. Their shudder, in our ironic sense, comes into the complexity of our distanced non-erotic shudder, one of our complex reactive moments.

At the dead center of the play, Ajax pauses to lock the dramatic irony by seeming to abjure what we know will happen. The speech has the contemplative and god-invoking ring of a chorus, and at the same time the poetic "swell" *(onkos)* of the messenger speech by which normally catastrophic events are rendered in Greek tragedy. In this play, by a bold stroke, the suicide of Ajax is given directly on stage after a shorter suicide speech that simply unlocks the dramatic irony and throws into a direct, silent present, the protagonists' death. It begins with brutal succinctness:

> The slayer stands, where may he become
> The best of cutters . . .                    (815–16)

In the earlier, central ironic speech, anticipation is deeply manipulated by the playwright into a general contemplation, just as later the handling of the event on stage keeps projecting the action forward. If the play followed Aristotle's prescriptions of "complication" *(desis)* and "unravelling" *(lusis)*, then it would be off-balance. But it does not do so, and the central subject is not exactly the suicide of Ajax, but really the management of the suicide of Ajax by himself and others— and by ourselves as this complex series is ordered into our passive awareness. The tonal unity of the play finds a thematic justification in the series which could not be discussed adequately without a much longer look at the structures outlined above. Meanwhile, the contemplative moment of the speech on time adapts the tension of our expectation to intensify and prolong its poetry:

> All things does time, the long and numberless,
> Produce when they are dark; when they are clear, it hides them.
> Nothing at all is unexpected. There is seized
> Both the dread oath and the all-toughened mind.
> And I, who just now held out so awesomely

Like iron dipped, was femaled in my voice
By this woman . . .
And when I find an untrodden piece of earth
I'll hide this sword of mine, most hateful weapon,
Digging the earth where it will not be seen.
No, let the night and Hades preserve it below . . .
                    So I must yield. How then?
Yes, for awesome and most powerful things must
Give way to honors. Thus does the trodden snow
Of winter yield to summer rich in fruit,
Night's everlasting circle stands aside
For the white-colted day to blaze its light . . .      (646–73)

One principle here (time brings all things to light) contradicts another
(I'll hide this sword forever), just as the declaration (I must yield to
the "honors" of the Atridae as winter to summer and night to day)
contradicts our foreknowledge. All such processes are subsumed in
the central one of voicing these expanding *logoi* at a point of the mythos
which remains so steadfastly given that there can be no question of
doubting Ajax either way. The speech can have no existence as a
natural proposition of intent, the way a speech by Coriolanus or
Richard II can; the mythos contains it, as the total dramatic performance builds the mythos through phases of a dreadful and persisting
question.


                                    3


The dramatic enactment draws into itself the significative constituents
of the context in which it begins. To gather for ritual purposes, and to
perform ritual acts in a series of which the play is one item, defines as a
base the kind of collective addressee that the audience constitutes. It
also homogenizes the presentation, and thereby something of the effect
on the auditor. The ritual identification of pity and terror, in the
diction of the plays, as well as in Aristotle's designation, may be derived from the fact that to see a Greek play was a stated corporate
obligation, just as the perceptual lingering impression of "woe" or
"wonder"—to turn the terms J.V. Cunningham[11] isolates away from

their scholastic sources—throws onto the emotional dimension of effect what can be tied to the condition of attendance at the English Renaissance theatre: the free, somewhat disreputable choice of the random spectator. The literary statement, as Meillet notes,[12] assimilates a common societal phenomenon to the ritual language out of which it grew in the first place.

The Greek audience (of whom we are presumptively a part when we attend to the sign system of a Greek play) stood close enough to those rituals to be aware that the members of the chorus were in some sense surrogates for themselves in more than a metaphoric way. Dance for Greece, as for other cultures, was a public and universal act, just as in primitive culture, music[13] is not the specialized activity of a class of musicians, but a function of each member of the culture.

Just as the rituals had a regional association along with their functional ones—Dionysus himself suggested the north and mountains—so the modes, Aeolic, Doric, and the like, had not only regional names but ritual and emotional areas of reference. These, in turn, get fused in the meters of chorus and lyric "interlude." What Jahnheinz Jahn says of the combinatory tendency of African music can be applied to the Greek modes used in the tragic choruses, in their shifts within one code or combinations in one line by *epiploke* and *sunartete,* "The polymetric basis of [the music of the drums] serves to allow a number of different beats to sound at one time."[14] Where the "beats" are "loas" (*lois,* laws), each a religious form-type, as the Greek modes are.

In the language as well as the music, a drama, like any linguistic act, exhibits powerful combinatory tendencies. All areas of discourse contemporary with the Greek drama—philosophy, historiography, law, even perhaps medicine, as well as epic and lyric poetry—are not only paralleled by the Greek drama, but assimilated into it formally through the diction, and sometimes through such characters as Prometheus or Xerxes.

The dramatic performance, in its character as a special, and institutionally virtual group gathering, assimilates easily to itself, by a kind of analogy which is formal as well as implicitly linguistic, the traits of the other, more specific gatherings in the society, not just Dionysiac cult gatherings but any assemblage of people. Like the law courts, it concerns itself with ethical questions and takes a vote at the end. Like the Panhellenic athletic games, it culminates in a group literary participation. Pindar, best known for his *epinikia* at games, also wrote dithyrambs for the Dionysiac festivals, a form that the tragic plays tended somewhat, but not entirely, to supplant.

The semantic function, as distinct from the anthropological fact, of this analogic contagion of audience-groups to other kinds of gatherings in a society, has been opened for discussion with the Renaissance theatre,[15] and we may interpret that theater's use of analogy to royal pageants and Church processions, folk festivals and schoolboy plays, bear-baitings and even public executions. So for the modern theater, the context of night club and film, to say nothing of other collective forms like the trial, the sermon, the lecture, and the panel discussion, are quickly assimilated as rhetorical shadows into plays: "the happening" can in fact be described as a dramatist's adaptation of the social form of "the party." But the only semantic function that has received serious discussion for the Greek drama is the law court,[16] and most of those who discuss the complexities of drama's connection with its own and other rituals bog themselves down in the prior question of the anthropological facts and their degrees of verifiability.

The semantic functions are complex because the Greek play combines as well as assimilates the forms it uses. Even in the choruses, the metric modes are not kept strictly discrete; they may flow into one another, as in lyric poetry.[17]

When the dithyramb is expanded to become tragedy, the iambic trimeter is imported so to speak, into the middle of the choric meters, to constitute the sole, staple measure of regular dialogue. This changes both the lyric harmony of the dithyramb and also the semantic functions expected for iambic, which until then had been mainly a satiric meter, though Solon, as Else shows, had turned it to a quasi-tragic use.[18] Semantically three transpositions have thereby taken place: (1) the dithyramb is modified by being made to assimilate a counterpart; (2) the satiric expectations of iamb, since they cannot be wholly abandoned, must be sensed as retained, but redirected and deepened; and (3) the ritual context is rendered problematic by the combination of (1) and (2).

The ritual, of course, is not thereby metatheatricalized: in no sense does it refer back to itself. We almost never have a play within a play in

Greece. The sacrifice needs semantic mediators to become a Sacrifice; Electra's reluctance (Eur. *Electra*, 175 ff.) prior to sacrifice retains its initial character as a natural human gesture when she confides it to the chorus, before it may be referred to other, abstract forms: it is a fact before it is a myth, the myth has accomodated the fact.

In one sense the Greek play is simpler than other literary rituals. At Delphi we have first the contest of the games, and then the Ode of Pindar. At the Greater Dionysia, the tragedy becomes the contest, and the restricted number of entrants stand to one another as the runners or chariot racers do in the Pythian Games: the outcome brings a winner, and the performance, like any contest (but not like any play in other cultures) is unique and never repeated. No one in classical Athens ever saw *Oedipus Rex* again, it remained forever a loser (though it grew in the mind of Aristotle who read it later).

But this recursive simplicity of the play upon itself—it provides its own occasion, while the games do not—coexists with, and provides a firm base for, a far greater complexity than that of a Pindaric Ode. An *epinikion* uses combined meters, and dances. It connects myths to a winner, to his given city of origin, to the actual games in which he won, to all Greece because the festival was Panhellenic; and it very often refers to poetry itself. A tragedy does all of these, except that the last such reference is confined to the exodos. But it splits the poet and the masked reciters, and it organizes the winner and his myth into changing triads on the stage, aligning the atemporal myth not mainly into flashes of allusion, though the choruses also adapt that aspect of Bacchylides and Pindar, but rather into a series of events. Paramount becomes the visible, purified ordering in time. Consequently, the means is given for other elements to be ordered into greater complexity, and while we may have only one city as a central reference in an *epinikion*, a tragedy often sets two or more into relation (Athens automatically as the site of the play). In the *Oedipus Rex* Corinth, Thebes, and Delphi stand conjoined to Athens and to each other. In the *Agamemnon*, Troy and Argos. In the *Phoenissai* of Euripides, those Phoenician women of the chorus become a gratuitously added group of transients, as if to insist on the possibility of this spatial multiplicity also, in a play that runs its virtuosity of mythic multiplicity through the entire Theban legend.

4

The soul's unconscious procedures are timeless in themselves, as Freud says,[19] and so are the myths that render their forces in figurative form. The Greek playwright, by placing the myth objectively in front of the silent spectator, fixes that timelessness, turns its ruminative vagueness into a kind of blank, and orders it into a pattern of time which teaches some deep sense of order. "Teach," διδάσκειν, though it means probably to teach the chorus its lines and gestures, is retained, surely because it carries some wider signification, as the regular word for what the playwright did when he put on a play. The order not only arouses the emotions "toward feelings of pathos," as Herodotus said of the tragic chorus,[20] but celebrates or honors them.

The play, in the simple unification of its presentation down on a circular stage, within the logistics of three actors at most, keeps the emotions unified too; it may break forth again and again in the simple monosyllabic cries of joy or distressed pain. Or it may stretch the bow of feeling (as of idea) taut in those exchanges which it formalizes in the regular one-line retorts of stichomathy, where the singleness of the metric unit dominates even over the dialectical doubleness of the form. Speaker A says a, Speaker B says b, setting b schematically into relation with what precedes and what follows, a and a.[1] But the stark, simple line holds a, b, and a[1] to a single tension.

The unifying of emotion involves a purification, and we do not have to solve more specifically what Aristotle means by catharsis to render it so. Plato[21] stresses how seeing a tragedy brings rejoicing and weeping together, in a context where he has said how fear, desire, wrath, and zeal *(phobos, pothos, orge, zelos)* mix in both body and soul.

All literary works posit an implicit dialogue marked by the suspension of normal response: the addressee cannot change roles with the addresser, as in natural language, and this suspension of his voice dams up the feeling which would release it. A dramatic performance brings the text alive, and then places it at a formal distance from the spectator, invoking the same condition.

In the dialogue across the stage, the audience absorbs the action in silence, reversing, as it were, the conditions of the analyst-patient relationship, in which it is the one "acted upon" (the patient) and not the "actor" (the analyst) who speaks. But the patient, qua patient, exists totally within a psychosexual framework of making accessible to the conscious mind the "Zuider Zee" of the unconscious. In what universe does the spectator dwell? Partly in a religious one, to be sure, if he is a Greek watching a play. And silence was interestingly a fundamental component of the Orphic mysteries whose rise may possibly have paralleled that of the drama itself.[22] The initiate was to keep an "ox on the tongue," the phrase from *Agamemnon* (36) that possibly echoes the mystery formula. Aeschylus, as Jaeger stresses,[23] grew up in Eleusis and stood trial for revealing the mysteries. The silence of the spectator, though, is only analogous to the silence of the initiate, even if both exist in the religious sphere. Enacted upon the spectator's silence is an otherness of evocative significances that bring to the fore his emotions for ordering.

The implicit structuring of emotion becomes explicit in the patterning of a Greek tragedy, where emotional responses are often paramount. It is emotional urgency, in masked single-mindedness, that purifies the sequence of time. Medea and Hecuba, Aeschylus' Clytemnestra and Sophocles' Deianeira, Jocasta and Oedipus, are all overwhelmed, beyond principles of primitive *dike* or civilized *nomos*. Euripides may well receive and incorporate the intellectual ideas of Protagoras and others, but Theseus, who at first refuses to listen to good arguments in the *Suppliants*, yields only to the simple appeal of his mother.

The play enacts. Finally, it presents not just the intellectual series of statements or positions, or even of coordinated actions, but the effect of all these on the silent spectator, something ultimately emotional, a catharsis.[24] For this catharsis his silence is necessary, a silence in the Greek sphere of both religious purport (to worship Dionysus) and of religious analogy (to practise the mysteries). The spectator's silence is also analogous in another way to the analytic situation: just as the analyst is all-powerful and the patient consequently childlike, or more precisely reenacting his childishness, so the spectator has enjoined upon him the silence of the child; it is children who are to be seen and not heard. But children, in their silence, desire to see what they can only hear, and their open eyes derive from the same situation as their closed mouths, the removal from the adult world, sexual in the Freudian scheme, but total on the dramatic stage, to which their emotions are being made aware.

So even in the *Antigone*, for all its careful balancing of reasoned
ethical opinions, it is the force of Eros and then of Dionysus that the
choruses invoke in their two climactic songs. Ismene remarks on the
feeling of Antigone, and Creon's first speech (280–314) at once distorts
his political principles by an admitted and verbalized feeling of
frustrated rage. His final state of collapse leaves emotion as the residuum of the play, and each of the play's three suicides is a by-blow
of impulsive emotional reaction.

To take a long look at another play whose patterning invites schematiz-
ing ideas, the *Philoctetes* is unified not by working out the ideological
positions of its protagonists, as commentators have implied, but by a
patterning of effects on the audience. The intellectual positions, like
the phenomenological handling of fire and space or the substructure
of myth in the play, serve finally to schematize the feelings towards a
significant trance.

Fire does play a part in the *Philoctetes*: Lemnos is (it was in antiquity)
a volcanic island and Philoctetes at a pitch of stress asks to be burned
in the volcanic fire (796–803)—a startlingly strong reaction. He has
the bow, in the first place, because Heracles gave it to him in return
for lighting his living funeral pyre on Mount Oeta. He moved by fire;
he is stationary by fire. And imaginary space also figures in this play:
the space that Odysseus dwells on in the opening speech, the cave into
which Philoctetes retreats and the rise over which Odysseus disappears.
Moreover, in everybody's mind, character's and spectator's alike,
stands the large Aegean space of the island, located midway (and hung
up also in the ten years of time) between the Troad, where the war is
being waged, and the Greek mainland, where Philoctetes hopes to
return. We are given an imaginary spatial triangle whose apex is at
Troy and whose base runs through Philoctetes' home country of Malis,
from which he has anxiously and vainly awaited word. The triangle's
two other sides pass through both the Lemnos that we see and the
Scyros where Neoptolemos claims to be returning. This triangle
provides a scheme for repeatedly invoked vectors of ironic motion or
stasis as the characters declare their intention to move in directions we
know are either fated for them or forbidden.

But to see fire or space as developing phenomenological units in no way forbids our taking them also as constructive elements in a mythic system, even for the *Philoctetes*, a play of the ultimate and condensed simplicity one might expect from a playwright eighty-seven years old after a long lifetime of superb production. The Philoctetes myth in itself is a simple one, standing at one remove from the Trojan cycle much as the wounded character himself does. The father, Poeas, has no involved story like Ajax's father, Telamon, and no renowned brother like Peleus. While Ajax appears some twenty times in the red-figure vases of the period,[25] Philoctetes appears only three times. That he was treated by each of the three great playwrights may be taken in itself to indicate not widespread popularity, but the paradigmatic simplicity of the story—though it connects to the Trojan War, Heracles, Achilles, Odysseus, and the chthonic forces surrounding the serpent who bit him.

Something, indeed, of the climate of isolation in the *Philoctetes* derives from its being an all-male play; that condition constitutes the ground of its feelings and a unit for it. By a kind of compensation, though, it is a goddess whom Philoctetes has offended, it is the embroil-ment of erotic entanglements that has led Heracles to be burned alive on a mountaintop, it is to the other goddesses, Earth (Ge), Cybele, Athene, Nike, and nymphs of stream and sea that the characters pray. Curiously, too, the chorus, in their one full stasimon, compare Philoc-tetes to the Ixion who sought adultery with Hera (676–80). A significant sexual dynamic may be described between Odysseus and Neoptolemos, between Neoptolemos and Philoctetes, and—following the order of the play—between Odysseus and Philoctetes. This dynamic runs beneath their intellectual positions; it propels their emotional reactions, and it participates in, but again does not fully constitute, the final impact of the play.

We do not have to look—indeed we cannot look—at the spectator's precise internal dynamic of emotion in order to understand what the play is performing thereon. We need only look at the play, but at the play as performative rather than designative. Nor should we look at it as an ultimately intellectual "synthetic absolute" or "significant form," though it may be so described; for that would be to see it only as an intellectual construct with certain heightened virtues of complexity and order. Rather, we should see it as it is performed, as a program for the catharsis of the silent spectator, a patterned series of emotional changes or even stabilities in the characters on stage which by reaction the spectator assimilates. Into that patterned series the special formal features of the play, its particular series of statements, are structured.

But if intellectual understanding, with Socrates and Freud, provides emotional liberation, then liberation in catharsis may provide understanding with Sophocles. As a spectator in the play, the individual merges back into the mass, and the myth receives a corresponding heightening to the second degree at the hands of the playwright, which allows the spectator supposititiously not just to share the unique vision of the playwright—though he does that as well—but to find himself a member of an idealized society of the purged, who exist not permanently, like the baptized or like Orphic initiates, but in a no-space and no-time of the final moment of the play. The enlightened spectator is a putative part of an enlightened society that the enacted play has created for that festival, but not just for that festival, because the literary work itself will cause the same effect eternally and with a connection to Dionysus that has its transcendence of Dionysus built into the very act of worship.

In the *Philoctetes*, Sophocles deals with such a tight situation in pattern and in fact, emotionally and intellectually, that we might be misled into thinking he played that tightness for all it was worth. We may at least guess that Euripides had done so, that he had worked the possible combinations among his three participants (with Diomedes instead of Neoptolemos) to the breaking point. Dio Chrysostom calls the *Philoctetes* of Euripides *poikiloteron*, more elaborate.[26] But Sophocles, as in the *Ajax* of perhaps forty years before, merely frames the encounters between Philoctetes and Neoptolemos by the presence at beginning and end of an unchanged Odysseus.

For the sequence, to begin with, we have at several points to presume an ideal emotional response. We cannot allow our spectator to like Odysseus, to despise Neoptolemos, or not to feel sorry for Philoctetes. We also cannot allow him the prior ignorance of the myth[27] which a modern spectator might bring to it and make it some other play. This is true for the large ironic shifts—the persuasion of Neoptolemos, the befriending of Philoctetes, his despoilment and rage, the restoration of the bow, and the *deus ex machina*. It holds, too, for the changes from speech to speech. Take the following sequence, almost the climax of the play.

"Is there nothing in it to change your mind back again" (1270)? Neoptolemos says to Philoctetes who has been crushed not only by being disappointed in his yearning to sail but also in having the bow stolen by his new friend. The friendship acts more poignantly on the responses of the audience, on its natural sense of justice, when they know that the friendship was feigned. Neoptolemos is in an impasse, but he holds the bow. The audience's final Olympian position of cathartic resolution is prepared for in time by the irony of its knowing that at last the impasse will somehow be resolved because Troy does indeed fall and Philoctetes, consequently, will indeed have gone back there. The curiosity of whether is replaced, through the dramatic irony, by the curiosity of how, and the audience's removal from ignorance of the final outcome releases it (makes it, as it were, less impatient) so that it can pay closer attention to the actual sequence of resolution. Or, since the fact of resolution is already known, it can pay attention to its justice, not alone to the intellectual justice, once again, but to the emotional rightness in the sequence. Its irony at once directs its attention toward, and places it magisterially above, the sequence, by compensation, as it were, for the childlike theoretic silence it has voluntarily and collectively laid on itself. The stichomathy so especially characteristic of this play serves not only to contain the intellectual positions in formulae but also to set their rhythmic expression into proportional equivalences; the irony is not only used but managed and structured in the artificial sound.

To continue with this scene:

PHILOCTETES
Such were you in your words even as you stole
My bow—arousing trust, secretly ruinous.

NEOPTOLEMOS
But I am not so now. I want to hear from you
Whether your view is to stay here and hold out
Or sail with us.

PHILOCTETES
Stop; speak no more.
For what you say will all be said in vain.

NEOPTOLEMOS
This is your view?

PHILOCTETES
Yes, and far more than I can say.
NEOPTOLEMOS
Well, I wish you had been persuaded
By words of mine, but if I happen not to speak
At the right hour, I have done.
PHILOCTETES
For you say all in vain,
And you will never put me in a friendly mind,
You who took my life away by tricks
And robbed me of it, and then came here to set
My mind straight, you odious son of a noble father.
May you all die, the Atridae most of all,
Then Laertes' son, and you.
NEOPTOLEMOS
Curse no more.
And here, receive these arrows from my hand.     (1271-87)


In this ultimate confrontation of Philoctetes and Neoptolemos we are
given no speeches of intellectual justification; that is implicit in the
hurt of each, but it is the hurt curse that Philoctetes voices, in answer
to the hurt appeal of Neoptolemos. Frustration dogs them; *maten,*
"in vain," (1276, 1280) is repeated. The duration (rhythmic and
temporal) of Philoctetes' persistent curse, as much as the fact, leads
Neoptolemos to break their fix. "Curse no more," he says in an
unembellished statement (1286–87). "And here, receive these arrows
from my hand." At this point he is released in so far as he has given in
to his sense of justice and we, the audience, are released by sharing it
(unless such simple responses can be attributed to the audience, the
play is nonsense). Similarly, Philoctetes is released from his frustration,
or will be, by having his bow back; and we with him. Yet, for this
release to take place, not just the linguistic gesture of the offer but a
corresponding emotional assurance must be forthcoming:


PHILOCTETES
What do you say? Are we being tricked a second time?

NEOPTOLEMOS
I swear by lofty awe for the pure Zeus.
PHILOCTETES
O welcome words, if what you say is true.
NEOPTOLEMOS
The deed shall be before your eyes. Stretch out
Your right hand and be master of your weapons.

[*Odysseus appears*

ODYSSEUS
But I say no, with the gods as witnesses,
In the name of the Atridae and the entire host.
PHILOCTETES
Child, whose voice is that? Did I not hear Odysseus?
ODYSSEUS
You did indeed, and you see close at hand
Him who will bring you back to Troy's plain by force
Whether the son of Achilles wants it or not.
PHILOCTETES
Not safely so, if this arrow flies straight.
NEOPTOLEMOS
Ah, by the gods, do not let the arrow fly.
PHILOCTETES
By the gods, dear child, let go of my hand.
NEOPTOLEMOS
I won't let go.

[*Exit Odysseus*    (1288–1302)

When the reassurance is given, Philoctetes takes the bow from Neoptolemos in a transfer that, while it provides the release for us to share in, pulls our irony tight in another overall question of how. All very well, our reactions may be imagined as asking, but if Philoctetes gets back the bow and hates everyone, how will he ever get to Troy (as we know he will) and Troy fall (as we know it will)? As though to answer the lacuna in our silent ironic front, Odysseus leaps forward, tremendously realigning the emotional status of each, and therewith the immediate "conflict" of response. We want the Trojan War to be brought to an end, but we do not want Odysseus to deceive the just youth or the suffering bowman. We are at the exact beginning of the

play: How can Troy be won, and at the same time justice prevail?
Odysseus stands for the first, but Philoctetes for the second, and
Neoptolemos, who has been trying to resolve the two positions by
working his way through our emotional responses to the point we know
will be reached, is now caught in the impasse wise Odysseus foretold.

Since we know Troy is won but do not know justice prevails, it is
toward the latter that our fear is directed. Philoctetes' next gesture is
to aim the bow at Odysseus, which is so wrong (since Troy can't fall
that way) that it supersedes justice. Neoptolemos again shifts position to
hold Philoctetes back; our reactions shift also, relieved that Odysseus
is checked, that Philoctetes' impulse can't take deadly aim, that
Neoptolemos is at least enabled to manage something small. But
Odysseus restores the initial impasse, it would seem forever, simply by
disappearing, as he had broken it by appearing. Nobody can "let go"—
a verb repeated once a line for three lines as he exits ($\mu\epsilon\theta\hat{\eta}s$, $\mu\acute{\epsilon}\theta\epsilon s$,
$\mu\epsilon\theta\epsilon\acute{\iota}\eta\nu$ 1300–1302).

Neoptolemos has no recourse but to resolve all feints and appeal
directly to the only resolving circumstance for everyone: Philoctetes,
if he goes to Troy, will not only help them but also heal, as well as fulfil,
himself. But in these terms Neoptolemos' formulation already contains
the grounds of Philoctetes' irrational refusal. "You are made wild,"
he says, "And you do not receive the one who brings advice"
(1321–22).

Not indeed, if it is a man.

But there is a *demigod ex machina*. In total unexpectedness to the
audience Heracles steps forth, throwing the emotions of all onto the
same plane, as Philoctetes and Neoptolemos are about to depart in the
wrong direction together. The demigod restates the arguments of
Neoptolemos in the same intellectual form but with wholly different
mythic, and so emotional, force; this appeal is in the mouth not only
of the demigod, but of the very one to whom Philoctetes owes the bow.
And Heracles begins his speech by inviting Philoctetes to consider not
his own sufferings but those of another, Heracles himself. His myth is
to work on Philoctetes somewhat as Philoctetes' is to work on us.

The *deus ex machina*, as a dramatic device, is not a quaint primitive
failing of the Greek playwright, but rather—in a linguistic modality
(myth) that does not admit of truth or falsehood—a means of meeting
the power of an impasse by a corresponding power of the very sort

that, in terms of Greek psychology, may have brought about the impasse in the first place. (No bow, no island; no Heracles, no bow.) Our expectations have been brought to an impasse here. On the one hand, the emotional sequence of the play, the resolution of justice, would be satisfied by the departure of Philoctetes and Neoptolemos in the wrong direction, along the wrong vector, for Scyros and Malis. But on the other hand, the sense of ultimate congruence which the play supports, the satisfaction of a proper completion which is always emotional as well as intellectual, would be frustrated if Troy were not to fall. Heracles objectifies a restatement of the resolving course, ending with an appeal to Zeus.

He begins by exhorting Philoctetes not to leave till he has heard his words *(muthoi,* 1410, 1417—stories also, since he tells his story). And he begins not in the iambic trimeter of ordinary dialogue but in the primitive choral measure of Doric anapests, a marching rhythm which mimetically not only reverses the collective feet of actors and chorus, but, so to speak, marches them off as to war.[28] They indeed pick up the anapests when he finishes, and that measure dominates the concluding dialogue, awakening in the auditor a sternness of martial expectation as they head to Troy along with the religious joy of fulfillment (we are at the festival of Dionysus). The last words, referring to the group, are an injunction to move with added female aid, that of the nymphs identified with the sea, who will watch over a journey spoken of in the play's last line as a "return."

χωρῶμεν δὴ πάντες ἀολλεῖς,
Νύμφαις ἁλίαισιν ἐπευξάμενοι
νόστου σωτῆρας ἱκέσθαι.

Let us then go forth all in a crowd
Once we have prayed to the nymphs of the sea
That they come as saviours of the return.    (1469-71)

This is the last of a series of acts of devotion to which the end of the play is given over, as though to relax gradually the tensions of implacability that had been presented in the main movement of the play.

The play structures the emotions of the spectators. Far from being obscure, or demanding depth analysis, these emotions are deducible, for the most part, without great effort from mere attention to the progress of the play: the force of the transaction resides in the plain sense of the language. To analyze the emotions further and specifically, would involve a relation between the spectator and the analyst. But much is coded into the language-construct of the play. Taking the pattern story of the myth, itself a structuring of emotional patterns, the playwright manipulates his language into a second pattern so that the silent audience can become aware of how the dynamic of a resolution may be recreated from the myth for a selfsufficient sector of represented action, a play.

There is a third patterning of emotion in the play, that connected with its musical accompaniment. The actual score, of course, and the actual figures of the choral dances, are lost. But we do have the metered choruses themselves, in their recursive strophic form, and in their cola associated with one or more staple emotional effects.

The switch from speaker to chorus or, in a speaker, from dialogue meter to choral meter, always betokens an increase of emotion corresponding to an increase of complexity for the meter. An increase of metrical complexity may be seen as a shift in expectancy, because more alternatives are offered from line to line: in the Aeolic measures of the play a glyconic may follow a pherecratic or other rhythm, and other dipodies may serve as a transition or resolution; but while a dialogue is maintained, iambic trimeter must follow iambic trimeter. The extreme case of the unexpected would be the totally ametrical, and this is exactly how the cries of pure pain in this and other plays function; for example the "aaaaa," with which Philoctetes punctuates (732 and passim) the conclusion (except for a couplet from Neoptolemos) of the one fully developed choral ode of the play.

Kitto[29] points out how the suppleness and lightness of the chorus in the *Philoctetes* serves the simple structure of this late play by keeping the chorus mobile in its dramatic function. More specifically, the relatively short parodos or entrance of the chorus (135–218) begins in "choreic hexapodies," to use Jebb's terminology, a measure quite close to the iambic of dialogue. They ask what to do and then go into glyconics for the praise of Zeus. But they are not left in this measure, into which they antiphonally resolve after Neoptolemos' answer. He replies to them in anapests, a Doric measure of quick processional march as a response to their Aeolic of aroused feeling. In this context the anapests, long silent from here on, look ahead for resolution to the anapests of the conclusion. But they reach toward, as it were, rather than exhibit, the Heraclean firmness. For Neoptolemos the martial anapests are a whistling in the dark of his and our perplexity as to how he can reconcile means and ends, or how, with his warlike purpose, he can face the man who ten years ago was left behind from the expedition of war. They also, as in other plays, betoken a general excitement.

The choruses throughout exhibit this masterly adaptability to the progression of the action. The playwright uses his sets of meters, with their heavy significative charge of emotional association, as an amplifier and also as a qualifier of his central linguistic resources. In themselves the meters are doubled sometimes and dovetailed, in a process the ancient metricians called *epiploke*[30] or interweaving. And in their relation to the text, they admit of many variations, only one of these being that of simple heightened restatement. The anapests of Neoptolemos introduce something that, emotionally and intellectually, is not worked out till the appearance of Heracles. The meter does this, and not what Neoptolemos says.

Or again, the meter may reinforce irony. The next chorus fulsomely utters the bacchics and dochmiacs of an emotion heightened into the paeonic meter. The goddess Earth is invoked for this male play, the Pactolus of golden abundance by contrast with the impoverished Philoctetes, and finally the Asian Cybele triumphant upon lions (391–401). But the sailors are doing this ironically over Neoptolemos's supposed loss; the heavy emotion is feigned, with the result that, in their ironic perceptions, the audience cannot help but redirect the heavy emotion. They feel an unfeigned pity that Philoctetes is the victim of feigning, the more so that the pity of the chorus is feigned. Still, by the time we reach the passage antistrophic to this one which corresponds, of course line for line metrically with the first invocation, the same heavy dochmiacs and bacchics express a pity this time unfeigned. In the steady confrontation of Philoctetes, the irony has been dropped, the chorus has now come to feel as we do; their pity serves as a direct, and not as a skewed, vehicle for our pity, invoking (this time with the help of metrical consonance between sound and sense, whereas before we had metrical dissonance) the further irony, again, of how the foreknown fall of Troy can come about if the sailors and Neoptolemos do not play along with Odysseus.

XO. οἰκτίρ', ἄναξ· πολλῶν ἔλεξεν δυσοίστων πόνων
ἆθλ', οἷα μηδεὶς τῶν ἐμῶν τύχοι φίλων.
εἰ δὲ πικρούς, ἄναξ, ἔχθεις 'Ατρείδας,
ἐγὼ μὲν τὸ κείνων κακὸν τῷδε κέρδος
μετατιθέμενος, ἔνθαπερ ἐπιμέμονεν,
ἐπ' εὐστόλου ταχείας νεὼς
πορεύσαιμ' ἂν ἐς δόμους, τὰν θεῶν
νέμεσιν ἐκφυγών.

Chorus
    Have pity, prince. He has told of many pains hard to bear,
    Miseries, as I hope no friend of mine may find.
    And, prince, if you do hate the bitter Atridae,
    I would turn their evil to the gain
    Of this man and would send him off
    On your swift, well-fitted ship
    Home where he wants to go, and so shun
    The nemesis of the gods.                                    (507–518)

Philoctetes has evoked this response not just by his piteous existence, but by his overt references to his father, to pity, to the eternal condition of man, and to the function of sight (three verbs for seeing, εἰσορῶν, ὁρᾶν, σκοπεῖν, 501–6).

But the chorus has the problem in its time scheme that the myth-knowing audience possesses on its atemporal level: how to avoid the fact that another fate is destined; how to avoid "the nemesis of the gods."

Even the simpler trimeters of spoken dialogue offer a range of possibility from curt (the stichomathies) to expansive (the long speeches). In these passages (500–50), in the flow of dialogue, the language tends towards the expansive, as always toward the emotional.

The gesture of pity towards Philoctetes, even in these relaxed measures, does not release the group on stage from the ironies they are permuting before us, and for us. Neoptolemos has ended his prior speech to

Philoctetes with what sounds like a straightforward injunction.

"Let us go, whensoever the god
May let us sail.                                                    (464–65)

In this statement there resides an irony toward himself (of self-
contradiction, of Odysseus' possible opposition, of his potential
acquiescence therein), and an irony toward Philoctetes (this friendly
offer after ten years of coldness will only increase the man's pain),
and an irony towards the god (who will never will that they go in the
direction of Malis), as well as in the form of the statement (it is ironic
in meaning the opposite of what it intends: the god does not have to
"yield" [εἴκῃ]; he always wills that they set sail, only in the other
direction).

As always, these ironies are towards us. In some sense all four of
them move through the passage at every point, and not just as the
entrance of the disguised sailor brings the always implicit Odysseus
forward before our eyes and those of Neoptolemos; but not those of
Philoctetes.

This play is about as schematic as a good play ever gets; it discusses
the question of ends and means in a simple form and with a minimum
of three active people. Yet their actions, presented before us as idealized
Greek spectators, only use this ethical question as a scaffolding for a
series of patterned responses to certain universals whose openness
comes through, and comes through only, in such series of emotional
evocations. Pain and loneliness figure here, youth and middle age, the
self and communal duty, and as always man and the gods.

The play's meaning involves not just a hypermythic[31] structuring of
emotion, free instead of fixed, individual instead of merely collective,
like myth. It also exists in time, and projects a dynamic sequence in
time. As we do, and do. It suspends our time and then reproduces it
in purified, and purifying form.

Language, like action, comes in sequence. The action of a play
cannot be divorced from the transaction of emotion on stage to the
plane of emotion in the audience, a plane that is different not only
because the audience keeps silent, but because what it knows and feels
must, in the conception, work differently from what one character, or
a series of characters, knows and feels.

The catharsis reenacts its phenomena as a management of a model history, leaving the management open as we turn away from the play. Philoctetes, Odysseus, and Neoptolemos, sail off together towards Troy, fixed in knowing what they must do. In working through the dynamic of their knowledge, we have turned typology into psychology, we are as free as they were at the beginning, but more empowered. Sophocles has charged our voluntary silence.

# Chapter Three: ATE

## 1

Le désir est la métonymie du manque à être.[1]

Le désir n'est ni l'appétit de la satisfaction, ni la demande
d'amour, mais la différence qui résulte de la soustraction du premier
à la seconde, le phénomène même de leur refente *(Spaltung)*.[2]

For an observer to stand by and see decisive, intimate actions, violates
the normal anthropological deployment of space, which assigns
segments of space to private groups, clans or clubs or families, and
protects by convention from intruding eyes what takes place among the
members. The Freudian primal scene would make the incest taboo
reinforce and causally explain this handling of *space* in any scene by
referring exclusions to a normal human handling of *time*, both physically
(what is past cannot be seen) and above all psychologically (we
should not look on at the congress of our parents).

The doubling in the theater between spectators and actors, the
reversal of the rule of exchange in speech dialogue, takes place, then,
on a charged ground where powerful rules are subverted. The new
space-time matrix activates the forbidden, while it realigns the space-
time of ordinary living.

The play, then, is intensely profane; and in Greece by being performed in an intensely sacred context, its tension between profane
and sacred—a tension inherent in the ambivalence of the *sacer* to begin
with—holds the problem of the sacred in balance. The problem itself
is made to yield intensifications in the sign-world of the play. In the
Renaissance that tension is skewed, in both England and (differently)
in France, where stepping out on stage is regarded—primitively, so to

speak—as a profanation to begin with. But any successful dramatic convention (and there are really so few!) must handle this strange, built-in tension and make it yield sense. A charged and heavily dangerous context obligates the play to match itself by producing an event sequence that brings to the fore an understanding of that very context. The meaning of a play finds the ground of the play as something of a source, a grammar for its message as well as an ordered context.

Within such limits it propounds what it may mean for limits to be transgressed. Greek tragedy deals not just with the fact of transgression, not just with the error (*hamartia* in all of its senses) of doing so, not just with the moment (*peripeteia*) when fortune (*tuche*) thereby turns on the recognition (*anagnorisis*) of the two. Beyond these terms lies the force leading to excess and error, the myth that is the pattern in the force, the *daimon* that is the source of the myth. And the play evokes the force while enacting a controlled perception of it, neutralizing it in the self unified with that other which is the sense of the myth transposed and sequenced in the presented play.

Only in dialogue with an other is the self unified, pulled together and propelled by an idealization of what it means to be in interactive relation to others. The self of the spectator, held by the stage barrier from the action, finds that collective other on the stage itself set into two groups governed by different laws: the single selves of the active participants, most like himself for being single and interactive, are stationary and *masked*. (The single reciters of dithyramb, a form coexisting with tragedy and continuing on into the classical period, were not masked.)

The second group, the chorus, is most like himself for being in a crowd (as at the moment he is) and being volatile of response, not strung into abstract, heroic extremities. The chorus may dance and sing, but must stay together, stay offstage a lot of the time, and come in only when the action is under way.

The tragic performance transposes onto the large scale of a formalized interaction a total life before the timelessness of myth and often before the actuality of death, ordering its statement towards what is the invisible Other by definition, the *daimon* which is the name for the power a god possesses before he is specified with the name of an individual god.

One set of doublings across the stage barrier may do duty for another: between the self and the *daimon*, the ritual and the unique event; even, as we abstract them, the doubling between the signifier (which the play also is) and the signified (by the play), between one moment of time and another, and between one kind of linguistic gesture and another: between music and language, between chorus and dialogue, between dancing chorus and stationary actors.

These doublings are reciprocal, and the pairings, with or without the middle term of the third speaker, build reciprocity formally into the interchanges of the Greek stage, which strain beyond reciprocity.

2

*Hybris* sets the act of going beyond a limit *(hyper)* into a spatial metaphor, and isolates it as a single, unconnected act. The term *ate*, however, (1) "madness," not only internalizes the excess by attributing it to a state of the person; it also carries suggestions (2) of a moral connection with some other act ("reckless guilt"), of (3) a "visitation" from some daimonic source, and (4) of a permanent condition ("ruin"). As Phaedra says in the *Hippolytus*:

ἐμάνην, ἔπεσον δαίμονος ἄτῃ.

I went mad, I fell at the *ate* of a daimon        (241),

where all the senses apply at once, as Barrett[3] comments. The "multitude of ills" is a "river," declares Pelasgos in Aeschylus' *Suppliants*, but the "abyss of *ate*" is a "sea" (κακῶν δὲ πλῆθος ποταμὸς . . . ἄτης δ' ἄβυσσον πέλαγος [469–70]).

As the opposite of *hybris* is *sophrosune*, a prudence that maintains the limits; so the opposite of *ate* is not health, but *soteria*, security or salvation. "Madness instead of salvation," (*Ant.* 105–6), Creon sees as approaching all the citizens. The absence of *soteria* pervades tragedy; it provides the hope, as *sophrosune* provides the technique, that keeps the tragic vision from being total even when, as within a tragic play, it is dominant. Oedipus comes on at the start as the "saviour of the state" (σωτῆρα) (*Oed. Rex.*, 48); but σωτηρία does not last, nor does the playwright's repeated invocation of the verb "save," through gods and mortals, do more than keep the hope alive.

If the gods were always malevolent at the end of the play, we would have no *dei ex machina*. At the beginning, some god must be so, or there would be no tragedy.

Athene opens the *Ajax* by showing the wise Odysseus how wrong things have gone, but all the good will Odysseus can muster does not operate to restore the balance of feeling that existed before he has influenced the judgement of the arms, driving Ajax into the rage that becomes *ate*.

> I hear your voice and seize it in my mind
> As of a Tuscan trumpet brazen-mouthed    (16–17)

he declares almost at once, but the trumpet does not carry. He pities his enemy for being "wholly wretched" (δύστηνον ἔμπας, 122), because he is "all tied up in an evil *ate*" (ἄτῃ συνκατέζευκται κακῇ, 123). And Ajax's bound condition binds the others even after his death, or else the play would have ended with that moment (or else be badly constructed by splitting in two, as some have ventured to say). "We who are not sick are caught in *ate*," Ajax's brother early says (οὐ νοσοῦντες ἀτώμεσθα, 269). Yet the *ate* is also described, like Phaedra's, as a "sickness," one "from a god" (θεία νόσος, 186). In this choral invocation to their generals for help, Agamemnon, too, spreads *ate*; "flaming heavenly *ate*" (195), the chorus declares while they wonder what god it can have been who struck Ajax down. Stating how his parents will bemoan his madnesses (ἄτας, 848) does not prevent him from killing himself, and the chorus then accuses itself of *ate* (909) for leaving him alone. Their final use of the word *ate* universalizes these extensions and spreads it through time:

> τίς ἄρα νέατος, ἐς πότε λήξει πολυπλάγκτων
> ἐτέων ἀριθμός,
> τὰν ἄπαυστον αἰὲν ἐμοὶ δορυσσοήτων
> μόχθων ἄταν ἐπάγων

What will be the last, when will the number of much
   wandering years ever stop,
Bringing the ceaseless *ate* of spear-hurling toils     (1185–89)

and the word assimilates to the "no man knows the future," of the
chorus's conventional closing sentiment, but not to any convenient
maxim that war is madness. The generality of the visitation in these
two lines keeps the "ruin" in *ate* from being derived just from the
"infatuation" or "sin" of individual warriors, or of an army, or of a
divine "visitation": it includes all these senses but cannot be located
comfortably in any one of them.


*Ate* has other senses than madness, and even that main sense posits
a more bewildering condition than those classified by Foucault[4] in the
stages of Western societal organization from medieval to modern times.
At each stage in our own culture, he shows, the madness exists and
takes on definition from the total dynamic of a transaction between
the mad and the nonmad. But in Greek culture, the madness totally
affects the individual without polarizing him towards his society. The
*mania,* a term sometimes used for *ate,* as in Phaedra's line above, may
have benign operations, as Dodds follows Plato in outlining.[5] *Ate*
always strikes one person, not a class of people. It is always presumptively momentary rather than permanent, though the disastrous
moment may take up much or all of the coherent action of a play. It
always involves the relation between a man and some god undefined
until ascertained. We know the reason because we have been shown
Athene at the outset of the *Ajax,* but the Salaminian chorus guesses
wildly and afield about Ajax's besetting god.

   *Ate* is always the most extreme and inward form of reaction to the
ups and downs, inevitable but not always devastating, of *tuche* and
*moira.* Beyond *hybris,* it breaks context wildly, it cannot be handled.
Oedipus Tyrannos has been bred a tyrant by his overweening, "hybris
breeds the tyrant" (ὕβρις φυτεύει τύραννον *Oed. Rex.,* 873), and he
can do no more once he is blinded and exiled but go on to a different
world. No such alternative stands for Phaedra or Ajax; in their *ate*
will be their end.

3

This word *ate*, not found in comedy or Attic prose,[6] manifests difficulties that history and philosophy gloss over. The tragic vision ascribed by Cornford to Thucydides[7] consists merely of a loose structural system or an anthropological echo, and also of a separate and optimistic wisdom: the abundant maxims in the speeches of Thucydides compress into a single phrase what in tragedy might take up a whole speech, but would also involve other dynamic relations, which Thucydides' concentration on his own theme must skimp; the cyclic mesh of power decisions allows for no other unknown. Not till the Romans will historians accord a dimension of tragic loss to the unique historical event.[8]

In the Greek view, the bare condition of fortune *(tuche)* without any special visitation of *ate* or mistake of *hamartia*, subjects a man's life to the likelihood of trouble. Herodotus, like any good Greek, assumes this, and he presents the assumption forcefully in the story of Polycrates of Samos,[9] whose friend king Amasis of Egypt wrote him to break his run of luck by choosing some misfortune. " . . . the gods are jealous of success, I cannot rejoice at your excessive prosperity . . . . I suggest that you deal with the danger of your continual success in the following way: think of whatever it is you value most—whatever you would most regret the loss of—and throw it away: throw it right away, so that nobody can ever see it again. If, after that, you do not find that success alternates with failure, then go on using the remedy I have advised."

Polycrates chose to throw a gold-set emerald ring into the depths of the sea. But a large fish swallowed it, a fisherman caught the fish and brought it as a present to Polycrates, and his servants brought him the ring.

When Amasis heard this, he replied, in the certitude of man's assumed subjection to *tuche*, "how impossible it is for one man to save another from his destiny," and he broke the pact he had with his friend. "This he did in order that when the destined calamity fell upon Polycrates, he might avoid the distress he would have felt, had Polycrates still been his friend."

Amasis' assumption was borne out. Failing to heed a prophetic dream of his daughter, Polycrates visited someone who murdered him and then hung him on a cross.[10] "I never heard of a man," Amasis had said in his first letter, "who did not come utterly to a bad end when he had good fortune (εὐτυχέων) in all things." (III. 40, 11–12). The word for "utterly", "to the root," (πρόρριζος) is as far as Herodotus can go with the assumption: history offers none of the tragic resources for exploring it.

Tragedy honors this principle, while going beyond it. To take one among countless examples, the ghost of Polydorus in Euripides' *Hecuba* stands over his unseeing mother to declare it:

$$\mathrm{\mathring{a}ντισηκώσας\ δέ\ σε}$$
$$\mathrm{φθείρει\ θεῶν\ τις\ τῆς\ πάροιθ'\ εὐπραξίας}$$

In counterbalance, some
One of the gods destroys you for your former bliss. (57–58)

Plato, who locates the question of happiness or its opposite in the goodness of the person, inverts this assumption without at all having recourse to the tragic complexity; he stays with the simplicity of Herodotus while propounding the opposite. After a discussion of nature *(phusis)* and law or culture *(nomos)*, he has Socrates say simply, "I call the good and noble man or woman blessed, and the unjust or pernicious one wretched."[11]

Between the fatalism of Herodotus' typical assumption and the moralism of Plato's call to virtue, the tragic poet finds a mystery, and finds given patterns of action to work into embodiments of the mystery. Where Aeschylus, in the tetralogies he was the last and perhaps also the first regularly to use, sees the mystery clear if the scale is cosmic enough, and where Sophocles propounds a deep piety of response to it, Euripides lucidly and enigmatically measures the mystery by presenting it as unmeasurable. In this sense, as Aristotle said, Euripides is "the most tragic of poets."[12]

He said it in a discussion of how tragedies manage *tuche,* and the word itself is one Euripides uses somewhat more than Aeschylus or Sophocles, even allowing for his having more plays extant than the other two.

*Tuche* names, from the point of view of hazard, the same principle that *ananke*, "necessity," does from the angle of certainty, and *moira,* "lot," or "fate," in the light of one man's share. *Potmos*, "destiny" too, comes round to the same ultimate view, which implies that all is in the hands of the gods. The words are almost interchangeable, and three of them *(potmos, tuche, moira)* appear as rough equivalents in this typical passage, as elsewhere:

> *XO. οὔτινά φημι θεῶν ἄτερ ὄλβιον, οὐ βαρύποτμον*
> *ἄνδρα γενέσθαι,*
> *οὐδὲ τὸν αὐτὸν ἀεὶ βεβάναι δόμον*
> *εὐτυχίᾳ· παρὰ δ' ἄλλαν ἄλλα*
> *μοῖρα διώκει·*

> I say no man without the gods becomes
> Blest or of heavy fate,
> Nor does good fortune enter always
> The same house. Now one destiny
> Pursues a house, and now another.
>                          Euripides, *Children of Heracles* (608–12)

The sentiment is to be found all through the tragic literature. As Amphitryon says in *The Madness of Heracles*:

> The fortunate are not fortunate through to the end,
> For all things stand asunder, one from another.     (103–4)

That play compasses the sundering by perceptive compassion.


4

*Ate*, when it comes in Euripides' plays, finds no countervailing force. For Hecuba, for the children of the maddened Heracles, there stands nothing like the Athene and the Odysseus, or even the Teucer, of Sophocles' *Ajax*.

Hecuba is maddened as a figure of the given myth: in her terrible grief she will be transformed into a bitch and fall from a mast into the ocean. The unremitting pressure brought to bear on her in the *Hecuba* should, then, for an audience who knows the myth, bring about this madness; but the main irony of the play transposes this action into a future prophesied by the Thracian king she has avenged herself upon. We never see her go all the way mad.

In the play itself she withstands pressure after pressure. Necessity is rigid (στερρὰ γὰρ ἀνάγκη, 1295), the chorus says, in the last words of the play, and the play exhibits that rigidity throughout, the unrelieved hopelessness of Hecuba somehow staving off the madness we had ironically expected to overtake her.

She is subjected, meanwhile, to other ironies, one of which dominates the first half, since the prologue is spoken by the ghost of Polydorus and the bereft mother thinks that son at least is safe away in Thrace. Then his dead body is brought in from the sea (681), where, ironically, she has sent a servant to get lustral water to wash the corpse of her daughter, the sacrificed Polyxena (780).

The maddening visitations are so constant that the word *ate* cannot emerge as a special definition in the play except on a single occasion, to name the doom of Polydorus:

ἔγνως γὰρ ἄτην παιδός, ὦ δώστην‹ε σύ;

Wretched one, do you know the ruin of your son?     (688)

And just before this she has touched her own closest point to madness:

κατάρχομαι νόμον
βακχεῖον, ἐξ ἀλάστορος
ἀρτιμαθὴς κακῶν.

I begin the Bacchic
Measure now that I learn
From the one avenging my ills.     (685–87)

The last of her ills, her forthcoming death in the form of a red-eyed dog, she will ironically hear as a prophecy, because Polymestor will have heard it from the Dionysus in whose measure, as she says, she says these words.

This is the climax of the maddeningly ironic series, where every point of *tuche* is sharp enough to produce *ate*. Up to the climax and away

from it lead other ironies: that she cannot even rise to enlist her sorrow
over Cassandra's concubinage to make an appeal to Agamemnon for
her other daughter's life; that when Polyxena has been slaughtered,
she must still appeal to him on those grounds, just so she may have a
chance at her enemy; that he will not even help her because, despite
justice, Polymestor is a friend and the Polydorus he betrayed is an
enemy; that the Odysseus who was once her suppliant will not help
her save Polyxena; that he will not accept her as a substitute, to say
nothing of Helen, who is guilty but ironically so close to her mother-in-
law as to have told her of Odysseus' disguise (243); that he will not
even let her die with her daughter; that Agamemnon answers her
appeal by saying he will set her free if she wishes, and she does not wish
freedom (759); that Polymestor pleads love and sympathy when he
enters and gets caught up in the irony himself of being blinded and
losing his sons for the same gold lust for which he killed Polydorus;
that she shuns his very rage instead of standing by to watch it
(1054–55); that Agamemnon himself finally (1247) is willing to accuse
him of a crime; that in the crushing last prophecies she must learn not
only of her own horrible end but that Cassandra also is to die (1255).
The end provides its own context of other ironies: Agamemnon's
false sympathy, Polymestor's false reason for killing Polydorus to protect
the Greeks from the threat of him, Agamemnon's refusal to believe the
prophecy of his own death.

The ironies, as they act upon an audience, fix the pathos of *tuche*
beyond repair. Under the aegis of an expected *ate*, they sustain a
condition so extreme that only rage, the last gesture of Hecuba, can
respond. The "rigidity of necessity," to insist on the chorus's last words,
has in it a flexibility, ever new in the particular ironic confrontations
it will produce, ever the same in the set condition of unreconcilable
encounters. Presenting *ananke* as irony has the effect of at once making
necessity inscrutable, since the particular combination is unknowable
to begin with (Hecuba lacks for the first half of the play the knowledge
that Polydorus is dead; for the last half she unconsciously resists the
madness, finally prophesied, which one who knew the myth came to the
theater knowing). It also has the effect of offering a law that can be
known as general, and yet a law that by definition renders one helpless,
since he is generally subject to the unknowability of the particular
combination. As the chorus says of the events of the play:

δεινόν γε, θνητοῖς ὡς ἅπαντα συμπίτνει,
καὶ τὰς ἀνάγκας οἱ νόμοι διώρισαν,

Awesome indeed how all things fall upon mortals!
And the laws keep defining the necessities.   (846–47)

Here *ananke* is given in the plural and the laws also, the *nomoi* to
which Hecuba has given allegiance in the depth of her distress:

The gods are strong, and so is that which rules them,
The law. For we perceive the gods by the law
And live distinguishing between right and wrong   (799–801)

This principle holds. Here we are never in any doubt (a question that
may be raised in the *Ion* or the *Bacchae*) as to what actions in the play
are right and what are wrong. But "the laws split the necessities," and
another principle that Hecuba enunciates will also hold:

Alas
There is no one among mortals who is free.   (864)

Odysseus, when he urges her to be wise (σοφόν) and to think (φρονεῖν,
228), is offering something that this very encounter proclaims to be
ironically inadequate.

   The condensed encounter, of which Euripides is a consummate
technical master, remains the irreducible vehicle of ironic interaction,
as when to soliloquize she stands aside from the Agamemnon who is
left standing in a power she craves and fears to beg (737 ff.), or as when
the blinded Polymestor, stunned by the presence of the crone who has
also killed his sons, turns the tables on her by activating the hidden
advantage of what blindness signifies in the Greek context, that a
seer is blind, and so prophesying her dreadful end.
   As she says, in the specific case of blood (shed):

The law lies equal for you, those who are free,
And for those who are slaves, in the case of blood. (291–92)

Ten years later, in *The Trojan Women*, Euripides returns to the same
mythic material and makes it produce the same vision on a broader
canvas. This time the prologue is given to a pair of gods, Athene and
Poseidon, the latter returning from the beautiful dances of the nymphs
to stand before an orchestra representing the ruins of Troy. They agree
they will soon destroy the Greeks, and the conquerors' upper hand is
then qualified ironically throughout the play by that particular
application of the same standard Greek principle that those who pro-
sper are bound to suffer. Meanwhile, Hecuba once more is to lose
Polyxena senselessly; her virgin daughter Cassandra is torn away to
serve the bed of Agamemnon; her faithful daughter-in-law Andromache is to be given to the son of the man who killed her husband; she
is to see the crushed body of her grandson Astyanax brought back;
and the woman guilty for it all, Helen, under the irony of Menelaus'
hypocritical shifts, is to be restored to the wronged husband who cannot
fully conceal his desire. The universality of subjection to suffering
heightens the pitch here; before that universality the chorus can end
with no real summary, however brief or grim. Its last utterances are
a bare, once repeated, monosyllabic cry of distress. In a recital of her
woes here, the last one Hecuba lists is that the dead Priam does not
know the madness, the ruination of her *ate* (1313–34), a term she uses
elsewhere (121, 137, 164) to name their misfortune, as does the chorus
(530, 535).

Women, at least in Greek society, as Hans Diller points out,[13] are
especially subject to events *(ta pragmata)*; and so Euripides makes them
his chosen vehicles of pathos, raising to a pitch the ironies of *tuche*. His
sympathy for women *in extremis* impressed his contemporaries, and
hardly a play lacks its woman overwhelmed by *pragmata*, from Alcestis
to Agave: Medea, Phaedra, Andromache, Creusa, Iphigenia, Electra,
Andromeda—even Helen in the *Helen* (see 255 ff.).

Mediating between nature and culture,[14] woman is at the same time
dependent on the world of men; she is torn by the complexities for
which they call the tune, even without Eros, of which she has the
deepest understanding, because she has had the deepest experience.
Hecuba, in the toils of her distress, applies erotic psychology to the
Menelaus of the *Trojan Women*:

There is no lover who does not love forever          (1051)

And it does not help.

In the *Hecuba*, her various functions—old woman, mother of
Polyxena, former beneficiary of Odysseus, widow of Priam—get in
each other's way. Prior relations that a man can handle, trip a woman
up in their contradictoriness: it does not help the dependent Medea
that she was once a princess, and the strength of the resolve that got
her Jason eventually causes her not only to lose him but to trans-
mogrify herself. From *ate*, she early says, "there is no issue easy of
approach," (κοὐκ ἔστιν ἄτης εὐπρόσοιστος ἔκβασις 279).

In *The Madness of Heracles*, the case is made of one who is not only a
man and an unusually strong man, but of someone whose origins and
final mythic function place him midway between man and god, a
demigod. Amphitryon stresses the connection, only to declare it is
"in vain":[15]

> O Zeus, in vain I got you as a co-husband,
> In vain I called you in common for our son.    (339–40)

He is about to be sacrificed, along with Heracles' children, and a wife
who touches on another legend that opens the prologue, Megara,
daughter of Creon and last descendant of the Theban house.

Their plight is desperate: they are in the grip of circumstance, as
they say again and again: Heracles has gone to Hades to get Cerberus
for Erystheus; and as Lycus says, arguing their plight, what mortal
ever came back from the dead (296–97)? The disparity between their
doom and Heracles' prowess is objectified on stage by a long choral ode
(348–450), coming at the point of Amphitryon's despairing resignation,
which lauds the labors of Heracles, success by success.

The ode also anticipates the unexpected arrival of Heracles himself
(514–22); but the whole series of despair–salvation turns out to be only
the first term of a tremendous preparation for the madness at the center
of the play. Heracles, after rescuing them all, slaughters his wife and
children because he is deluded into thinking them Erystheus's. The
logical substructure of his loose end, that he has not delivered
Cerberus,[16] becomes the line of fault which breaks him into a *mania*, a

rage that may be "diagnosed" as epilepsy[17] but that is brought on by a goddess, Lussa (rage).

The presence of Lussa on stage and of Iris with her, (822 ff.) brings to sight a set of conditions far more overwhelming, even for a hero, than the murderous hostility of a merely usurping king like Lycus. The madness in the myth has a cause, an ancient grudge of Hera. In the play it constitutes an incursion into a troubled series; we have seemed to reach the end of trouble, only to be at the beginning once more. The horror of *ate* has got beyond language, the chorus says, repeating the word in its transfixed helplessness:

> πῶς παισὶ στενακτὰν ἄταν ἄταν
> πατέρος ἀμφαίνεις;

How shall you show the lamentable
father's madness, madness against sons?　(917–18)

Heracles, though taken away to Athens by Theseus for the glories of his last apotheosis, cannot recover from his grief, and he sees himself as under taboo for his *ate*; he uses the word in the plural:

> οὐ γὰρ ἄτας εὐπροσηγόρους ἔχω.

I have afflictions no man can approach and speak to　(1284)

The chorus, too, concludes in a moan of sorrow. The first restoration from misfortune has worked: Heracles puts down Lycus; but the second cannot: who can restore the children of Heracles?

Euripides changed the given myth[18] by putting the infanticide at the end of the hero's life, as well as by adding Lycus and Theseus. *Ate* thus becomes the cornerstone of the enacted life.

Nothing further can be expected that is not named in the play. Heracles' despairing wish to have his flesh consumed in fire (1151) introduces the legend of Nessus' shirt only by allusion, in a modality of no actualization. His only relief, a temporary one, has been the great stone Athene pushed against his chest to put him to sleep after his murders (1003–7). He carries his cosmic disturbance to the Athens to which Theseus invites him and where the play is shown.

The greatness of the protagonist, his seeming invincibility, finds its temporal dynamic counterpart in the plot's gigantic double take: despair, rescue, deeper despair.

*Ate,* the final agent of misfortune, is displayed as far more savage than any military conquest or explicable human grudge; it breaks even the close calculations of the historian and the philosopher, and so they do not use the word. It was left to the tragedians to keep the term from Homer as an axis of connection between man and gods, the inner world and outer world, an axis leaving the connection incalculable and inexplicable, but demonstrable in the presented contemplation of a dramatic enactment.

# Chapter Four: TELOS

First of all, there is darkness in the starting point of our speech. We would not begin to seek light in speaking if we were not conscious of a lack of light. Darkness can be a beginning of light only if we are aware of it as darkness . . . .

Secondly, there is darkness also in our speaking itself. Speech brings to light, but we do not know how . . . .

The third reason why there is darkness lies in the fact that in our reflections upon speech we become aware of the important role played by the body . . . .

Speech tends to eliminate its own incoherences. Its search for coherence is facilitated by the fact that speech itself implies a kind of reflection, a placing of oneself at a distance.[1]

## 1

The rite of the festival is an eternal return, every year the same. The enactment of one play at the festival locates another order in the return, the order of the lives that are under pressure behind the masks and that find that their conclusion *(telos)* defines their purpose *(telos)*[2]; one end defines the other end; and for both ends the seasonal ritual, in all its finalities, serves only as a first term and a context.

Over the coherent span of one play, to which Sophocles is later willing to confine his dialectic, Aeschylus builds the tremendous arch of still another order, the trilogy. The large overarching order of the trilogy stands to the small order of the single play as the small order of the play stands to the incomprehensible, and so ritualized, order of life (in its one small, significant part, the festival of Dionysus). As Finley says, "The trilogy as a form is more revolutionary than tragedy as a form . . . when this heroism stands in a trilogy, it becomes more than itself; it both denotes a character and is a stage in a progression leading to a farther and higher state of being."[3]

The trilogy points beyond its own ultimate state: the Eumenides only begin at the end of the *Oresteia* to become those benign goddesses Athene has invited them to be. Antigone at the end of the *Seven* is locked in the *telos* that constitutes itself a new problem, the very one to which Sophocles devotes a play.[4] Even if we had the last two plays of the *Prometheus* trilogy, the future they would declare would be, in the given terms, unimaginable.

The end of learning-by-suffering (πάθει μάθος, *Agamemnon* 177) abrogates the vast counterbalance of *dike,* the scales of justice. Still, *dike* is universal; and so that end, which the long time of the trilogy brings round even at the span greater than the single life, cannot be imagined in the life that must learn by suffering. It is not exactly a mystery in Hathorn's terms,[5] as the dominance of a god would be, something inexplicable but known. Rather, the end must be what the progress of the long-range action deepens under the word *telos. Telos* is light on a darkness of what cannot be known because it has not yet come to be. "All" in Aeschylus, as Kiefner points out[6], serves as a term to "unveil." What is unveiled is that ultimate state which the whole trilogy in its logos has elucidated, but must lie beyond. And the urgency of the thundering Aeschylean style strains toward the beyond it has resigned to a state lying at the other end of its end, beyond the suffering through which alone there can be learning, in the justice that has to get through to an end not wholly to be seen in its counterbalances. Omnipotence, freshly named Zeus, will itself, inconceivably, age into a just counterbalance *(dike)*, even if the Titan who declares that end is buried out of sight at the edge of the world's tallest and remotest mountains.

In the *Suppliants,* the first play of its trilogy, what the Danaids ask is granted, asylum at Argos; but it does no good: their counterbalances of female against male, Greek against Egyptian, refugee against attacker, will not hold against the larger counterbalances of the long destiny shadowing the race of Io. They must create that *telos* themselves, they must violate the counterbalance of justice to murder their husbands on their wedding night—all except one, Hypermnestra, who emerges, in the counterthrust of long stresses, as "fulfilled," presumably (τέλειος, 8), the way the woods are, and the heavens and the earth, in the one fragment we have left of the last play.[7] Her fulfillment occurs in a state so normal it is remarkable that it should have taken so long.

The *Seven Against Thebes,* as the last play of its trilogy, reduces the long stresses of the Theban house to a confrontation which is at once simple (fighter against fighter), undeniable (the defense of a city), reciprocal (brother against brother), and unresolvable—except by the death that engulfs the two brothers. But the city is saved. The main presentational force of the play is tied up first in prayers, mainly by the chorus, and then by the great set speeches assigning heroes to each of the enemy heroes at the seven gates.

The main motion finds its end in the salvation of the city. But there stands a slightly larger motion that dominates the conclusion of the play—the heroes die in defending the city, and the dead are mourned; and the sorrow takes precedence even over the joy of victory. These motions, the victory and the sorrow, exist within a still larger causality, the curse uttered by Oedipus himself, not only on the Theban house in general, but specifically on Eteocles and Polyneices for warring brother against brother. That opens up, at the play's end, a completely new problem; the trilogy looks again to the deadlocked intransigence of Antigone (assuming the end to be genuine), which sets the just-unjust equation into the new dimension of life and death. The *Sphinx,* the added satyr play, would surely not have opened this particular end further. It remains an open end, the present universe of the kind of moral problem posed by the city where Aeschylus lived—and the city where Sophocles lived who took this very subject as the set problem for the *Antigone* not too long afterward.

Compared to the *Suppliants* and the *Prometheus,* the simple, antagonistic center of the *Seven's* finale to a Theban trilogy is reductive; the city is reduced to an armed camp; the Army to Eteocles, an intermediary, and six other champions; all questions are reduced to the single question of outcome. Nor is suspense offered; the victory is announced flatly in a single line before its details are amplified in the more traditional set messenger speech. The long poems of choral lament, the tight elaborate speeches, one for each hero, of trumpeted assignment, beat their wings around the cage of these reductions.

The cosmic range of the *Prometheus* trilogy is counterweighted by the first action of the first play, the one we have: the Titan is nailed down in the Caucasus by the incarnated principles of Zeus' power, Force and

Might. Thus he is subjected to the law he voices:

τέχνη δ' ἀνάγκης ἀσθενεστέρα μακρῷ.

Skill is far weaker than necessity.                    (514)

He stands for skill, as Zeus for necessity. Being subject to the gods, the Titan resembles humankind; and yet to the same degree that Zeus exceeds him does he exceed the humankind whom he had rescued from their feeble existence. They are spoken of—though not brought on stage—as lacking the very quality of forethought from which Prometheus derives his name.

Prometheus, the superhuman embodiment of human skills, stands both metaphorically (since the skills are human ones) and metonymically (since he stands to man as benefactor to recipient) as a living transposition of suffering into unimaginable learning, in the unimaginable end of a future beyond the skills that are all that can be directly named. Heracles, a man who becomes something more than man, will be the agent, this play tells us. The language of the fragments from the middle and concluding play hints at something other than skills: "the justest place . . . of all mortals . . . the furrows bear for mortals an unwearying life, the whole land is soft, and Zeus pities you when he sees you helpless"[8]—Zeus who here feels no pity.

In *Prometheus Bound*, the necessity superior to his superhuman skills involves a sequel to a prior cosmic interchange. The children of Heaven (Ouranos) and Earth (Ge) have been supplanted by the grandchild and then the Titans, by Zeus. Around the immobilized Titan, Prometheus, other forces interchange, more or less powerful, but powerless beside the all-powerful: Oceanus appears to help, Io (who carries the seed that will seed into Heracles) to complain, Hermes to domineer. Typhon and Atlas are mentioned but do not appear.

Against the long aeons of these cosmic actions the vision of a humanity-before-Prometheus is unfolded to the humanity now in the audience:

First of all those who could see saw in vain
And the hearers heard not; resembling the forms
Of dreams, in a long life they confounded all
The likenesses and did not know that houses

Could be brick and face the sun, and knew no woodwork.
They dwelt in underground tunnels like swarms
Of ants in the depths of caves without the sun.
Nothing there was for them a definite
Sign of winter or flowery spring, or fruitful
Summer, but without intelligence
They did everything, till the risings of the stars
I showed them, and the settings, which are hard to discern.

(447–58)

An enormous gulf had been crossed between these men lacking intelligence (*gnome*) and the Athenians who were watching the play. The play projects that past into a visible, mythic present, as a way of projecting that present into a future whose indiscernibility already exists as a necessary condition of the transition from past to present.

The possibility of Heracles, inconceivable to Io, stands for a remote end, that Heracles could accomplish, a cosmic labour attributed to him nowhere in mythology but here: the abolition of what without the mighty emotional logic mounted by the Titan's play would seem a condition no end could dissolve:

There is no one free except for Zeus     (50)

The play, faithful in its structure to the allegorical sense of its protagonist's name, looks ahead toward the future, to the "term" of the events, as well as to the apocalyptic *telos*. So he says to Might:

ποῖ ποτε μόχθων
χρὴ τέρματα τῶνδ' ἐπιτεῖλαι.

wherever the ends
of these sufferings must finish off     (99–100)

And the chorus repeats it to him:

πᾳ ποτε τῶνδε πόνων
χρή σε τέρμα κέλ-
σαντ' ἐσιδεῖν.

wherever
you must sail and see the end
of these labors                                                   (183-84)

But the play ends as he sinks under the earth, in the dramatic stance
of not knowing what he has been declaring will come about, the end
of a remote future. He concludes with "I suffer."

Still, for him as for the humans he suffers through having helped,
lack of foreknowledge is an important counterweight to the presence of
foreknowledge. He has given men not only the skill of forecasting, but a
central ignorance which is tallied in with the other gifts. Not knowing
when he is to die, a mortal is centrally limited in whatever other foreknowledge Prometheus may have given him:

Θνητούς γ᾽ ἔπαυσα μὴ προδέρκεσθαι μόρον.

I made mortals stop seeing in advance their doom.     (248)

He took away with one hand, then, what he gave with the other. His
own *telos* in the trilogy magnifies the mortal spectators' sense of their
own *telos*, less titanic in its range but more total in its compass.

His act rings the change of inversion on the main proposition: as
past man to present, so present Titan to future free Titan. Here, paradoxically, to remove the foreknowledge of death is to give something;
and so to suffer will somehow result in a future of nonsuffering; long
time removes sacrifice, but potentially not within the span of a mortal
life.


2


The time span of reference in the *Oresteia* is expanded from the origins
of the Trojan War (*Agamemnon*, passim) and the feud of Atreus
(1583-86) to the present of the enacted play, since it ends by instituting
an existing judicial procedure. The expansive reference, however, is
brought to bear on a simple set in counter-balancing *dike*: one murder
wipes the slate of another murder, except that these simple conditions

immediately expand into the past and future. It takes the sacrifice of Iphigenia, and so the condition of the Trojan War, to explain why Clytemnestra will murder Agamemnon. His son, to wipe the slate, must incur another guilt; the only way out of one bind is into another, since the murderer of his father is precisely his mother. The psychodynamics of this situation, and—what concerns Aeschylus—its judicial modality, takes the whole procedure mounted in the *Eumenides* to get out of the bind. The end is deadlocked until a new element can be introduced to break the deadlock. The renaming of the Erinyes immobilizes the whole procedure into a single term, Eumenides, or a cluster of terms: the holy ones (σεμναί), the maidens (κοραί). By this rededication, the dramatic momentum plunges ahead into a ritual procession of celebration; the whole urgency of the process implies that mere naming cannot settle, any more than mere adjudication can. Theodicy cannot come about in the contracted world of judicial balances, any more than it can in the *Prometheus'* world of intellectual propositions and cognitive skills. The *dromenon* is needed, the larger *dromenon* of the trilogy. Learning is by suffering the longer span.

The presence of the Erinyes haunts the language of the first play (*Agamemnon* 59, 463, 749, 991), the term taking a prominent place[9] in each of its choral odes. Orestes at the end of the *Choephoroi* can see the Erinyes who are invisible to the chorus and also, presumably, to the audience who are their surrogates. When they do become visible in the play to which their altered name furnishes a title, their presence is powerful enough to drive the action to a different location—towards the center, so to speak, where the play is being enacted, towards Athens.

The imperative they present, of avoidance or some horrific dissolution, mobilizes the conflicting questions that the judiciary cannot fully handle, and that therefore must be loosed by fiat for the future to operate at all. There is a conflict, the central one, between right and wrong, unresolvable because Orestes has done both right to avenge his father and wrong to kill his mother. He did so at the behest of a god, an act that mobilizes still another conflict, the one between men and gods, a perplexing one because a god can do no wrong. The gods are either malevolent or benevolent, that opposition providing still another conflict, which is resolved by turning the gods of extreme malevolence, the pursuing Furies, into figures of kindly benevolence. Moreover,

Orestes' impasse is not a simple logical impasse. It implicates and
transfixes in his own psychic economy, the social history embodied in
immemorial codes of matriarchy, or patriarchy, and of their tense
interplay. The opposition between the female Furies and the male
Apollo sets the conflict between male and female on the plane of the
gods. The further divine figure who resolves this conflict is a female who
has male attributes, Athene. She carries a device, the "aegis" mentioned in the play (*Eumenides*, 404), of a horrific beastly severed head, the
Gorgon, that may be taken to stand for her "suppressed" femaleness.
Psychoanalytically, the writhing snakes of a female head may signify
the "mother-with-a-penis" of transfixing depth fantasy, and the blood
may be menstrual blood. Athene, then, redistributes, in manageable
form, the bestial and awesome female characteristics of the Furies,
who are themselves more than once called Gorgons (*Choephoroi*, 1048,
*Eumenides*, 48). She is benevolent towards Athens, as they become
towards Orestes.

The conflicts are resolved when the transposing dramatic actions
move them to a point beyond the central situation, as they had been
moved from a point well before it. The long end is so wide in its
parabola from the long beginning that the *dromenon* outruns the
*legomenon*.

3

Poetry, when it is put in the mouths of speakers on a stage, aligns its
intensities toward their purposes; it becomes oriented toward an end;
consequently, its moments, moment by moment, are weighing the end.
The dramatic statement responds to the pressure of the past and presses
on to the fulfillment of a future. The verbalization of a *telos* comes
through in the last chorus of the *Oresteia*, the procession at the end of
the *Eumenides*:

> Σπονδαὶ δ' ἐς τὸ πᾶν ἔνδαιδες οἴκων
> Παλλάδος ἀστοῖς· Ζεὺς Παντόπτας
> οὕτω μοῖρά τε συγκατέβα.
> Ὀλολύξατε νῦν ἐπὶ μολπαῖς.

> The oaths are for all from co-dwellers
> In the city of Pallas. All-seeing Zeus
> And Fate have thus gone along with it.
> Shout now with the melody.                    (1044–47)

What the all is that "all-seeing" Zeus sees is indicated in the previous sentence as a fusion of some completeness (τὸ πᾶν), objectified into an abstraction that can take the article, with an end-directed purposiveness which the preposition (ἐς) signifies: time and the end of a time at a stroke, an end encompassed for human beings as seen by Zeus. By Zeus, and also by a Fate the trilogy has referred to throughout. The unification implied by the verb that joins them (συγκατέβα) performs a verbal act of coordination which Bruno Snell has noticed in tragic language generally: "Again and again compounds with '*sun*' crop up; so important is the notion of togetherness, of common action and perception."[10]

The last word, sung in a sort of dance, refers to both dance and song, present as they are viewed by the audience, but again aimed toward a celebration of something future as well as something past. The moments of these words, centering on the "*νῦν*" of the last line, are inextricably bound up in the span of the trilogy over its *telos* and beyond. Whether in chorus or dialogue, the intensity-points of poetic statement bring the *telos* to bear upon the moment, as well as expressing the moment itself.

In the *Seven*, the ominous sense of coming war culminates in the assignment of seven warriors one by one to oppose the appropriate enemy chieftain, an action that from its first announcement occupies the center, and half the time, of the play (283–676). Each of the highly wrought set pieces describing the enemy heroes climaxes in a poetic fact: the emblem on the shield of each. The poetic fact spurs the dramatic decision, because Eteocles in each case chooses the appropriate combatant on the basis of an intuitive reading of that emblem. Within the poetic statement itself, the emblem serves both metaphorically to signify the hero and metonymically to concretize his military essence, since the shield is the "warring part" of the hero, and since the emblem would have to have been not an accident but a deep choice of self-expression, metonymic then (and metaphoric too) of the hero's ethos.

The sixth assignment moves this process to a dramatic silence because the seer Amphiaraus, who is quoted as having himself made a long set statement (580–89), bears upon his shield not an emblem but a blank. The absence of a shield device is defined as the desire to move from seeming to being:

σῆμα δ' οὐκ ἐπῆν κύκλῳ·
οὐ γὰρ δοκεῖν ἄριστος, ἀλλ' εἶναι θέλει

And there was no sign on his round, (shield)
For he wishes not to seem, but to be, the best.        (591–92)

Eteocles at once responds to this as to an excess of madness:

ἄτης ἄρουρα θάνατον ἐκκαρπίζεται

The field of *ate* yields the fruit of death.        (601)

But there is a reach left beyond the blank shield—that of uncertainty—which covers the seventh warrior he will face himself, his brother Polyneices, for whose shield a double transposition is effected: from known (blank or otherwise) to unknown, and from a picture to the letters that are conjectured as possibly standing on it:

ταχ' εἰσόμεσθα τοὐπίσημ' ὅποι τελεῖ,
εἴ νιν κατάξει χρυσότευκτα γράμματα
ἐπ' ἀσπίδος φλύοντα σὺν φοίτῳ φρενῶν.

We shall soon know where his emblems end
If gold-wrought letters babbling on his shield
Shall lead him forth in his wandering of mind.        (659–61)

In the perspective of *telos*, (τελεῖ) Polyneices is imagined (but not known) to move haphazardly out of—and also into—an incoherent and impulsive language "boiling up" (the metaphor buried in φλύοντα) on something, letters, that would stand for him (if they existed) because he brought them into expression.

Here, and more strikingly in the *Prometheus* and the *Oresteia*, the language rises to figure. Yet the Jakobsonian categories of metaphor and metonymy will not fully classify the splendid verbal moments rigged in the amplified voice of the masked actor. The structure, or substructure, has been transcended, by being fused at a high pitch or confused in the pell-mell rush. For ordinary language Lacan[11] can retranslate the displacements and concentrations of the linguistic and Freudian dreamwork into a generalized system of manipulations whereby the "bar" between signifier and signified is either maintained, as in the contiguity–combination of metonymy (if "sail" means "boat," the sail must touch the boat), or erased, as in the similarity–substitution of metaphor (if "swan" means "boat," the boat must move out of the language to be replaced by the swan).

The implications of this process for a speaker who is thereby remaining silent about something while speaking of it, provide Lacan with a model for the underlying subject in all psychological transactions. And so forcefully for the amplified transaction of dramatic speech, all of which taken as a whole is both metaphoric (the performance stands for something) and metonymic (the actors and the chorus are in a special sense, as members of the same society, cousins as well as surrogates of the audience).

The Aeschylean moments of intensity keep poetic language at the magnificent level of displaying this fusion in dialogue and in chorus. When the guard, in the prologue of the *Agamemnon*, declares,

> ἄστρων κάτοιδα νυκτέρων ὁμήγυριν,
> καὶ τοὺς φέροντας χεῖμα καὶ θέρος βροτοῖς,
> λαμπροὺς δυνάστας, ἐμπρέποντας αἰθέρι

> I know the concourse of the nightly stars
> And those that bring winter and summer to mortals,
> The shining powers illustrious in the air            (4–6)

the amplification of his last line has the ring of a metaphoric crescendo. Yet in the conjunction of "shining" and "powers"—aside from its being the first in the play's code of significant lights all the way to the torchlight procession ending the *Eumenides*—we have something that is at once a metaphor (the strength of powers is seen as a light) and a metonymy (at this obscurely early time, the stars can be called powers only if they are seen in relation to the forces of the gods). They (1) "stand out" in the "bright air" *(aither)*, to which they are also (2) "fitting," being (3) "famous" by implied metaphor like the athletic heroes to whom the word *"emprepon"* is also applied. All of these senses not only condense but enter into combinations of metaphoric possibility with the powers and the bright air. The prephilosophic Greek offers elisions of linguistic function comparable only to our most advanced poetic strategies; the dramatic situation objectifies and protects them into a sequence that is purposive as well as poetically significant. The bow is always being strung taut to shoot the words towards the final signification of the *telos*.

So too, the chorus's backward look in the long cola of the opening ode tell us something about themselves while sending the rhythmed verbal sequences as long probes into why they are where they are. The two eagles tearing the hare of the portent that Calchas interpreted stand for Agamemnon and Menelaus destroying Troy, but they must be interpreted by Calchas in order to mean that. As a real point, an event witnessed by the Greek Army, the comprehensive metaphor of the omen touches metonymically on the sequence of the war—and on the consequences being brought before our eyes and ears first here in the words of the chorus. The eagle, however, is also the bird of the Zeus whom the chorus will soon invoke; it has a double function, as Finley[12] points out: "Agamemnon is originally Priam's prosecutor; he is the eagle who avenges the despoiling of its nest (the theft of Helen by Paris) . . yet . . .the eagle who kills the innocent hare." And the choral poetry not only carries these complications but displays them by the force of its conjunctions.

> οἰωνῶν βασιλεὺς βασιλεῦσι νεῶν ὁ κελαινός, ὅ τ' ἐξόπιν
>     ἀργᾶς,
> φανέντες ἴκταρ μελάθρων χερὸς ἐκ δοριπάλτου
>     παμπρέπτοις ἐν ἕδραισι,
> βοσκόμενοι λαγίναν, ἐρικύμονα φέρματα, γένναν,
>     βλαβέντα λοισθίων δρόμων.
> αἴλινον αἴλινον εἰπέ, τὸ δ' εὖ νικάτω.

The king of birds to the kings
Of the ships, the black and the one dazzling behind,
Hard by the house on the spear-hand side
In all-conspicuous places,
Eating the brood of the rabbit teeming with many young
Injured from the remaining runs.
Call woe, woe, let the good win out.          (114–22)

The athletic runs, the pregnancy, the spear-hand side, the kings, the black and the shining, all differ in their metaphoric set among themselves and from what they are centrally describing, the (metaphor, and metonymic event, of) hare and eagles. Touched into the poetry also are the archaic expressions which bring the dignity, and eschew "humbleness" as Aristotle recommends[13]—and also by old language recall old events, "ἴκταρ," "ἐρι-," "ἐξόπιν,," and "αἴλινον" itself.

The rhythm of invocation takes the refrain of the last line here away from the abstractions of which it is composed. Its fidelity, in the capsule of one sentence and a single long metrical phrase, to the whole *telos*-resurgence of the trilogy (an inextricable woe gives way to the inexplicable victory of the "well" of both prosperity and virtue) keeps it from sounding like an oxymoron. The dramatic progression, between what the audience knows (Orestes will be harassed) and what it doesn't (he will be saved by Athene), holds it above these merely verbal contradictions.

The whole is with us at every point. When that dominance has become clear, entire choral cola will be repeated verbatim toward the end of the *Eumenides* (788–92 equals 803 ff., 837 ff. equals 870 ff.). The language has moved toward the identities it has strained for all along.

The metaphors even of the peerless Pindar, by contrast, hold their intensities within the given frame:

Χρυσέα φόρμιγξ, . . .
καὶ τὸν αἰχματὰν κεραυνὸν σβεννύεις
αἰενάου πυρός. εὔδει δ' ἀνὰ σκά-
πτῳ Διὸς αἰετός, ὠκεῖ-
αν πτέρυγ' ἀμφοτέρωθεν χαλάξαις,

ἀρχὸς οἰωνῶν, κελαινῶπιν δ᾽ ἐπί οἱ νεφέλαν
ἀγκύλῳ κρατί, γλεφάρων ἁδὺ κλάϊ-
θρον, κατέχευας· ὁ δὲ κνώσσων
ὑγρὸν νῶτον αἰωρεῖ, τεαῖς
ῥιπαῖσι κατασχόμενος.

Golden lyre . . .
You quench the speared thunderbolt
of ever-flowing fire. Zeus's eagle sleeps on his staff, slackening
quick wings both ways,
lord of birds; you shed a black-faced mist on his hooked head,
sweet lock of eyes; dreaming, he ripples
his liquid back, held
by your buffets.            (Pythian I, 1 ff., based on Lattimore)[14]

All the terms connecting the lyre to the bird of Zeus, and Zeus himself,
order their complexities simply. So with the profound aphorisms:

ἐπάμεροι· τί δέ τις; τί δ᾽ οὔ τις; σκιᾶς ὄναρ
ἄνθρωπος. ἀλλ᾽ ὅταν αἴγλα διόσδοτος ἔλθῃ,
λαμπρὸν φέγγος ἔπεστιν ἀνδρῶν καὶ μείλιχος αἰών.

Of a day! What is one? What not? A dream of a shadow is
Man, but when the Zeus-given gleam comes
There is a shining light for humans and a honeyed age.
                                    (Pythian 8, 136–39)

These terms stand in an austere simplicity of signification, for athletic
victory, for banquet, for poetic statement, in and of the age of a life.
Not just in Aeschylus at his most sublime poetic moments, but in
dramatic verse generally, the *telos* of the action tends to draw the poetry
out of an emblematic set, or of a disjoined maxim. Here, for example,
is Medea at the moment of soliloquy:

ἀλλ᾽ εἶα· φείδου μηδὲν ὧν ἐπίστασαι,
Μήδεια, βουλεύουσα καὶ τεχνωμένη·
ἕρπ᾽ ἐσ τὸ δεινόν· νῦν ἀγὼν εὐψυχίας.

ὁρᾷς ἃ πάσχεις. οὐ γέλωτα δεῖ σ' ὀφλεῖν
τοῖς Σισυφείοις τοῖσδ' Ἰάσονος γάμοις,
γεγῶσαν ἐσθλοῦ πατρὸς Ἡλίου τ' ἄπο.

But let it be. Spare nothing of what you know,
Medea, you who plot and exercise a skill;
Creep to the awesome. Now is the contest of soul.
You see what you suffer. You should not incur ridicule
From these Sisyphean marriages of Jason,
You who were born from a noble father and the Sun
(401–6)

It would be curious to describe the even movement here as a progression of mixed metaphors. As in the opening succession of three verbs for knowing, each formulated moment offers its own whole universe of response. The humbleness and animal despair of "creep to the awesome" immediately changes to illustrate awesomeness by invoking an athletic contest, an agon, of a soul well enough to be in balance and thoughtful enough (through the verbs of knowing) to use the abstraction. Sisyphus, whether the line be construed[15] as having him image Jason or parallel him, provides a whole structure of relationship to Jason (like Sisyphus in being a newcomer to Corinth, a usurper, whose wife did what Medea is later to do, etc.), but not to the Sun, another and separate universe in its moment. Here linearity is a triumph of measured dramatic time and not a primitive, paratactic condition of metaphor. The verse sweeps on to the *telos* of the action.

4

The naturalness of the responsive interchanges of dramatic confrontation, too, are swept up to be set in the larger span. When Agamemnon's self-mastery struggles with weariness before the carpet, when Clytemnestra so luxuriates in sexual jealousy before Cassandra that she is deaf to her prophecies, when she taunts her husband with how Iphigeneia will meet him in the underworld, when Aegisthus finally dares to appear and then boasts of a daring that his contingency belies, no real light is thrown on motive. These vividly natural intensities take their light from the great, simple progression which is itself natural, and itself on the same plane: vengeance and purification may be internalized, may exhibit their own moments of natural response. They differ from weariness and jealousy, resentment and daring, only by theirparticipation in a larger *telos*. Vengeance and purification take in the span of a life, and more than a life, the span of the trilogy.

The language stands to the action here as a manifest content to a manifest content:[16] it speaks about itself without the brooding implications of latency that dominate the language of the modern theater. An act does not underlie a speech latently, as in Chekov, or differently in Beckett. Nor does the manifest poetry display the inner dynamisms that a Shakespearian speech often bodies forth. The act latently underlies a larger act, by being drawn into its larger open pattern. The "fusion of the superhuman and the superstitious" that Hermann finds[17] in Clytemnestra's last speech may be attributed to the whole trilogy. So may the mood he attributes to the opening speech about the beacon lights, "a magnificent undertaking that indicates at once a bold spirit and a passionate longing," though the longing voiced by the Herald will be fulfilled not at once, but only after two murders and a divine resolution have sent forth the calm torch bearers of the final procession.

In the *Agamemnon* a woman sacrifices a Warrior King and a Divine Prophetess, but the archetypal set disappears in the end of the play. The agony of confrontation with Cassandra, lasting far longer than the murder, does not make the play a "lyric tragedy" in the easy catch-phrase of some commentators. It invests its effect in the exhaustive probe that gives this one stage in the trilogic series the intolerable time to bring its agonies toward some conclusion, for some other *telos* to supersede.

The supersession comes first in a change of personnel. The *Agamemnon's* chorus of old men (a man is murdered) gives way to the *Choephoroi's* chorus of female captives (a woman is murdered; Electra is a kind of captive), and these human groups give way to the chorus of Furies in the *Eumenides*, who are themselves changed in nature midway through the play; the dramatic operation is so powerful that it can transform the very choral group, it can reverse the function of divine beings.

Among the characters, of the seven in the *Agamemnon*, only Clytemnestra and Aegisthus reappear to be killed in the *Choephoroi*. Of the seven in that play, only Orestes reappears in the *Eumenides*. The three who have reappeared, taken altogether, form the *dike* group of the central situation.

The very last action of the *Eumenides* presents a completely new group, the processioners who are far closer to the dramatic spectators in their nature and function than any of the other three choruses had been.

They, and Orestes, are the only persons appearing in the play who do not have some sort of status that transcends normal human existence. The other two humans who appear are a prophetess-mouthpiece of Apollo and the ghost of his murdered mother. The action comes about between Apollo and Athene on the one hand, and the Furies on the other. It has been driven to this divine plane by the perplexities of human retaliation: the effect is not of moral exploration, but rather of transcendent categorization. Human ends, confounding themselves, refer to ends more than human.

The language, of chorus and dialogue, expands into straining amplification, over and beyond acts that come quickly and almost wordlessly: the sudden arrival of Agamemnon, his sudden death, the sudden arrival of Orestes, his sudden acquittal. On the real scene and on the imagined scene, the suddenness takes the objective form of some physical presence or references whose emblems it does not dwell on because the language is so fully preoccupied with other matters: the torches, the carpet, the bathtub, the libations, the lock of hair, the foul-winged maidens on the altar, the lots in a helmet, the torchlight procession. Overriding the mere purposiveness of human action, the speeches tend toward prayer, with which the trilogy begins and ends. (And Aeschylus dramatizes prayer generally, as Schadewaldt[18] points out.) The first word of the *Agamemnon* is "gods," and the second "I pray" ($\alpha\grave{\iota}\tau\hat{\omega}$). The *Choephoroi* begins with a ritual procession; so does the *Eumenides,* which also begins with a prayer.

The long entrance ode of the *Agamemnon* casts its vision backward in the form of a prayer, and Cassandra's extended utterances of prophetic vision, like those of the prophetess who opens the *Eumenides*, stand in obedience to Apollo. Beyond such visions are the dreams that haunt the recollections of the play, the long dream of Clytemnestra of the serpent suckling a "clot" (θρόμβον, *Choephoroi* 533) in the milk from her breast. Orestes declares that this dream will bear its *telos* (τελεσφόρον, 541). Torches (537) have vainly been brought in to dispel this dream, which has impelled a vain prayer (538). The ghost of Clytemnestra (*Eumenides* 94–116) says she will haunt his dreams, and says it vainly. "Fear is a clear interpreter of dreams," the chorus wrongly says in its fears (*Choephoroi*, 32–33).

The end of the whole envisions a condition broader even than the kledonomancy described by Peradotto[19], than that of the visions and dreams it includes, and more dynamically purposive in its relation to the gods than the prayers in the trilogy, or the prayer at the festival of the trilogy itself, may find correspondences for. The final torchlight processions are "dancing" ritually towards a common life subsuming vision and dream, act and acquittal, in a *telos* that is a complex beginning.

The herald at the beginning, because he must watch for the beacons, has no dreams (*Agamemnon*, 13). But his torch is only a *symbolon* (8), a token whose most common form is the shard broken in half and shared by guest-friends. The other half of this *symbolon* is not one other torch, but the whole complex series of torches that blaze from mountaintop to mountaintop across the length of the Aegean, as Clytemnestra ecstatically describes it in the longest speech of her first appearance (281–316), ending on the word *symbolon* (315). All the many torches that get lit in the course of the trilogy can be taken for completions of the *symbolon*. This first completion is an ironic one, indicating hostility and not friendship, exuberant duplicity and not calm convention, spanned distance and not memorialized proximity. The last completion of the *symbolon* consists of the calmly moving, gathered lights held by the singing procession at the end of the *Eumenides*. The wild torches of the beacon signal, spread across the civilized world's peaks, exist on the imagined scene, but they cannot be seen; they are only named. The calmly ordered ones at the end, gathered in the hands of a single surrogate ritual band, are visible, having become so through the teleological sequence of the enactment.

5

For all the *Oresteia's* tremendous leaps in space and time—from the expedition against Troy to the homecoming of *Agamemnon*, from one end of the Aegean to the other, from Delphi to Athens, from a legendary past to the hypothetically coextensive present of a shared judicial procedure—it stays within human life and does not probe what comes after its end. It ponders the justice of murder, not the sense of death. Except that it occurs in the festival, it does not broach the dark side of Dionysus, the dying god.

Nor can we imagine that its satyr play, the *Proteus*, did so. The title gives no such hint, the few words preserved from it tell us substantially nothing, and anyway the satyr play, so far as we can tell from vases and the little evidence we do have, emphasized the fertile side of Dionysus, not the dark side, sex not death. The satyr play of the Danaid trilogy tells the story of a playful rape, and the satyrs of the conventional choruses wore phalli.

But Euripides, in the first play we possess by his hand, the *Alcestis*, quizzically reverses this convention and does address the question, as well as the fact of death. What is more, he does so in a play which was given in place of a satyr play. He thereby added the puzzlement of what death means in the context of a genre supposed to celebrate sexual union, where the only character approaching a satyr, reminiscent of the drunken Dionysus, is the drunken Heracles, who often appeared in comedies and satyr plays.[20] Moreover, it is just he who brings Alcestis back from the dead.

Sex does enter the play, in normal marriage, which is immediately referred to the central condition of the fable about death.

In normal life a man does not know when he is to die. That key fact of the future is hidden from his gaze; consequently, he cannot erect any sort of sacrifice convention to deflect the ultimate blow. Moreover, unless he incurs illness or violence, he will ripen past his prime into death. King Admetus is a healthy man in his prime, and he knows when he is to die, thereby violating both these conditions. A special, fabled relation to the gods allows him, uniquely, to offer a substitute. The one person willing turns out to be the person in a family most immune from any possible sacrifice, let alone this impossible one, the wife,

Alcestis. The play thus reverses the usual conditions of personal and representative death, itself a reversal.

Death, the end of life, then, reverses the conditions of life. That reversal finds ritual expression in Greek culture as in others. Nobody was allowed to cross the threshold of life, to be born or to die, on the sacred island of Delos. No one was permitted to be killed while the ship on an oracular visit *(theoria)* there in memory of Theseus was under sail.[21] The dead, as Thomson comments about the expired Agamemnon in the *Choephoroi*,[22] receive laments as joys *(charites)*. In doing so the dead powerfully reverse the responses of our lives, and this makes it hard to get through to them. The meaning of life itself in the world below may be reversed, according to a fragment from the *Polyidos* of Euripides:[23]

τίς δ' οἶδεν εἰ τὸ ζῆν μέν ἐστι κατθανεῖν,
τὸ κατθανεῖν δὲ ζῆν κάτω νομίζεται;

Who knows if to be alive is to die
And dying is considered living, down below?

All actions in human society occur in a pattern of reciprocity; even the willing sacrifice, the scapegoat, stands in reciprocity towards the gods. The death of Alcestis, however, since it is a substitution rather than a sacrifice (it is attended by no other ritual than mourning; it has no communal dimensions), constitutes a unique event that cannot really be matched or consequently understood. Every encounter in the play may be seen as an attempt to locate the sense of a death that in violating the ordinary conditions of dying raises by its uniqueness, but in a displaced form, what the sense of death in general may be. The deified character Death, who argues with Apollo, pleads that his rights have been violated by the substitution.

The question raised by this particular, strangely anomalous death, casts a long shadow on other elements in life, including the ritual for the dead, which seems so exaggerated here, since it is undermined by the fact that the chief mourner is also the chief beneficiary. This fact, which no diminution of the status of women in ancient society can nullify, must mute and distort toward something approaching satire the protestations of Admetus. The farewell scene, though reminiscent of the farewells on Attic grave stelai, cannot be taken wholly straight. When Heracles enters and is received in guestship by the mourning king, the question of propriety before the corpse within immediately comes into view. The points argued between Admetus and his father about filial duty, and about old and young, are seen in the light of the fact that Alcestis has presumably already died; therefore, the question is moot of whether the father or mother should have taken her place in taking his, and their discussion oddly stalls.

The death tests the self of the king, and the question of sexuality, so warmly and pathetically raised in the lament of Alcestis herself, takes on grotesque proportions in the face of her husband's hardness. Sexuality, of course, is exactly the area with which the satyr play concerned itself, and in that way the strange *Alcestis* remains in the convention. Admetus vows never to remarry, but a statue replica of her (346–52) will lie in their bed for him to embrace, a provision that freezes the stiff figures on stage in the irony of an unperceived unnaturalness. The final test is a sexual one: he has to face a warm and breathing replica of his wife in the person of the veiled figure led in by Heracles at the end.

The demigod, who has stopped off here in Pherae between two labors, has been able to do more than the god Apollo. Because of two prior deaths (Zeus killed Apollo's son Asclepius; Apollo killed Cyclopes in revenge and had to serve the mortal Admetus for a year in punishment), Admetus was able to prove himself so pious that he got the boon of postponing his death by finding a substitute (1–20). Apollo was in a position to reward the "piety" of Admetus (ὅσιος, 10) by an offer which will not so much test that piety for endurance, since Admetus never really falters, as put it in this totally questioning light. Heracles resolves the question by restoring Alcestis, not through a judicial contest like Apollo's but by "snatching him in ambush" (1142).

The position in the play at the end, after all this dialogue—and dialogue preponderates in the progression of the utterances—remains what it was in the beginning. Such a reversion, again, is strange for the enacted time-series of a play. But the whole sense of death's reversal of life's conditions has been explored, through exhausting the emotions and presuppositions of the king. Thus deepened, he, and we, have reached an end that is identical with the beginning only in its outward conditions. The *telos* is only, and so quite purely, deeper than the beginning. Using a word (μεθηρμόσμεσθα) which may signify trans-posing into a different musical mode or tuning a lyre, he says in his last statement that the result has been not just a restoration of his prior life but an improvement:

νῦν γὰρ μεθηρμόσμεσθα βελτίω βίον
τοῦ πρόσθεν· οὐ γὰρ εὐτυχῶν ἀρνήσομαι.

For now we have changed over to a life better
Than the one before. That I'm lucky I'll not deny.

(1157–58)

"Many are the forms of demonic things," the chorus then chants. In this form the end of the dramatic enactment has been a transposition which is somehow a restoration. The whole play may be drawn through that single verb, μεθηρμόσμεσθα; the end changes the sense of death, and nobody has died. The silent audience has been brought up to, and through, an end that changes nothing. Mortality has been reassured through the process of restoring it only to the fact of its own existence, a circle it cannot break, tragically or otherwise.

# Chapter Five: NOMOS

A la *monarchia* un régime *d'isonomia* est substitué dans la nature comme dans la cité.[1]

## 1

*Nomos*, law, is the same word as *nomos* a musical mode. In the Greek vocabulary the idea of patterned recurrence and the idea of constituted principle unite in a single term. So *harmonia*, the fitting together of parts, signifies a musical accord too: and *rhythmos*, a regular musical recurrence, also means a proportion among ordered elements of any sort. *Isonomia*, equal law, which occurs as a term at the historical time when monarchy is going out, places both ideas within the political realm: *isonomia* means equilibrium among forces, but also the principle that gives a citizen equal rights in a democracy.

Tragedy propounds the *nomos* of a divine law by patterning the *nomoi* of musical modes, and metrical speech, into an ordered segment of enacted time. The myth itself is timeless in two senses: first the myth universalizes, in a timeless relation, the particular fact of some event in time. Second, the events of a myth itself, in their significance, are indifferent to the temporal ordering they may be given: "the character of organized totality that every myth offers," Lévi-Strauss defines it, "in which the unfolding of the tale makes explicit an underlying structure, independently of the relation between before and after."[2]

The tragic play takes the time-neutral material of the myth and directs its sequence into an order of significant time. The universal is invested with the quality of mortality; gods do not die, the myths resist time, but human beings succumb to time. Time after time, in a trilogy.

Tragedy thus transmutes the indifferent into the inexorable. The myth can always be retold, but in the single, rigorous progression of a dramatic performance the end remains the end, and not just a point of reference for the beginning. Jacqueline de Romilly[3] remarks that the word *chronos*, time, occurs four hundred times or so in extant tragedy, and very haphazardly in poetry before.


The time of tragedy objectifies its submission to the universal principle of *nomos* by being ordered into a *rhythmos*, a proportion among its segments of time.

The moments of division, if measured by who is speaking, can be located externally in the traditional parts of the form that Aristotle lists,[4] *prologos, parodos, epeisodia, stasima, exodos*, with the *kommos* sometimes added. But each play, and presumably each trilogy, offered its own *rhythmos* or patterning of events, varying these externals so freely as to throw the pattern of the action-in-time into proportional relief. In the *Suppliants*, for example (whose form we can no longer deprecate by dating it as an early "primitive"), we have no *prologos* and no specially significant *exodos*. For the remaining three regular divisions *(parodos, epeisodia, stasima)*, the action is ordered so as to overlap them heavily. First, overlapping the *parodos* and the first episode, there occurs the dialogue about Zeus and prudence, between Danaus and his daughters (1–233). Second, the daughters and their father plead with Pelasgos for refuge (234–523), an action that includes parts of two *epeisodia* and at least one *stasimon*. Third, the original group, in two more *epeisodia* and perhaps two *stasima*, contemplate the previous action (524–824). Finally, the Aegyptioi arrive, presenting their united pressure in another series of alternations between dialogue and chorus (825–1073).

The action, then, is not packed into the neat packages of the external divisions: rather the parts of the action and the formal divisions of the tragedy shadow one another; the *rhythmos* of their proportional relation doubles the more powerfully because the correspondences between them are only accidentally exact.

So too, and more splendidly, in the *Oresteia*. In the *Agamemnon*, which is dominated by choral meters, the Expectation, the Arrival, the Contest, the Murder, and the Justification all draw the formal divisions into themselves. Of these sequenced events the Expectation takes up proportionally almost half the play (1–809), heavy as it is with the past. The Contest between Cassandra and Clytemnestra and its aftermath (1035–1342), heavy as it is with the future, lasts longer than the Arrival and the Murder taken together. The imbalance of these proportions sets the central event, the Murder, onto a plane where a vastness of time dwarfs the short action in itself, while magnifying it in its isonomic relation to the larger law of action that the play is ordering.

The middle play, the *Choephoroi*, is dominated by dialogue, not chorus; by a presentness of dialectical confrontation and not by the ruminative absorption in past and future time. Once again Arrival, spanning *prologos*, *parodos*, *epeisodia* and *stasima*, is given far more space proportionally (1–837) than both Murders and their Aftermath (838–1076).

The last play—though it closes off the sequence and ought, so to speak, to be looking to the past—looks instead even more to the future. Dialogue and chorus stand now in an equalized, proportional, alternate relation to one another. The action is divided neatly into a proportional triptych of Pursuit at Delphi (1–234), Trial at Athens (235–751), and Acquittal with its aftermath (752–1047), the middle part taking half the time and the first and last dividing the other half between them. The *dromenon* of instituting law is made to establish an even symmetry to the action's units of time, *nomos* as principle being exemplified by *nomos* as pattern.

2

As the larger divisions of the action distribute the implied laws of preponderances in time, so the smaller moments, objectified for the reactive perceptions of the audience, respond to the hidden forces of the time in whose law of before and after all the agents are involved. To call those hidden forces "turbulence" with William Arrowsmith,[5] is to emphasize their capacity for stirring things up, a necessary prelude to seeing how the given play promulgates the law of what those things are, while providing a *nomos* to manage the turbulence.

In the *Trachiniai*, Sophocles, the Apollonian master of proportion, orders his dire events into four episodes and four *stasima* of comparable duration, between a long prologue of Deianeira as she waits for Heracles and a long *exodos* as the dying Heracles orders his son Hyllus to heap up his funeral pyre and then marry Iole, the princess who has caused so much distress.

But the expectation of Heracles' arrival, postponed for the fifteen months of his service to Omphale and his expedition against Eurytus, is carried through the first three-fourths of the play, till his entrance at Line 970. And by this time his consumption in the shirt of Nessus has led everyone to believe him already dead. The desire to which every character is subjected (πόθος and its verb occur 9 times in the play) takes on a rhythmed equivalent in this long wait, a suspension that binds the audience into a removed version of the intolerable span.

Deianeira's anxiety about the disintegration of a fragment from the enchanted shirt is cut short, however, before this, and at once, as their son Hyllus announces prematurely the death of Heracles. The occasion of the announcement is furnished with the conventional dramatic circumstance of a messenger speech, the lengthy set piece of elaborate poetic description after the short blow of the delivered fact (749–820).

Messenger speeches, which practically always recount a death or some other violent event, duplicate, by the heightening and prolongation of their language, the sense of awe that the convention of having the death take place offstage is honoring. The tension of that special silence produces a special amplification of dramatic speech, and something of the awe round the dim anthropological echo of Dionysus' ritual death is met by something like a liturgical recitation. But here all this significance operates only to turn the screw further. It breaks by anticipation; it cannot await longer the true, even more horrendous, rhythm of the guilty hero's death.

The domination of the stage by Hyllus' particular monologue does homage, by its unusual length and special poetic heightening, to the pressing sense of fate no man can overcome, a point made twice just before this, by Hyllus:

> What has come clear, who could make it as though it had
> never been?                                                    (742–43)

and by the chorus

> One must not judge what is hoped before it happens  (724)

The action overdetermines this sense of fate by holding the events at this high pitch. We are given, in staccato succession, still another messenger speech, a true one, announcing the suicide of Deianeira in her bedroom (899–946), the double-take that the mutilated Heracles still lives (974 ff.), and Heracles' final injunctions to Hyllus that he see to his father's death and marry his father's mistress.

Still, between each of these events and the next, the proportions of the prolonged opening are maintained by choruses that space the blows with lyrical meditation. That underlying regularity is preserved, as the rhythm of blow after tragic blow is stepped up.

In the interruptions of proportion, Sophocles manipulates a Deianeira far more virtuous than the rough murderess of the myth and the etymology of her man-slayer name, as Errandonea shows.[6] Yet he argues that she is guiltier than the plain facts of the play can allow this abandoned wife to be, who uses a love charm and then kills herself when she learns how its effects have gone awry. The given myth of the heroic Heracles is also manipulated so that he heartlessly creates stress for his family before he is finally shown to stand heroic stress himself.

Words for time abound in the play, but predominantly in the first half ($\chi\rho\acute{o}\nu os$ twenty-one times, $ai\acute{\omega}\nu$ and compounds three times, $\kappa\alpha\iota\rho\acute{o}s$ once, $\acute{\alpha}\epsilon\acute{\iota}$ twenty-five times). Desire has gone under to time: Deianeira, who emphasizes in the prologue how she had suddenly been enabled when young to choose the young Heracles as an alternative to the old Achelous, stands now at the point where she is old and Heracles is attracted by the young Iole; the princess, in turn, will lose the hero and gain his young son, because the old wife made a tragic error, one induced by still another rough suitor, the Nessus whose love-charm shirt is really a death trap. The regularity of the presentation, like the schematism of these correspondences, is disrupted by another, unpredictable order, under the Zeus who is responsible for all, in Hyllus' final words. As pattern, and the subversion of pattern, do duty for motivation, so the superimposition of an irregular climactic series upon a regular time sequence does duty for fate.

The taut encounters of Sophocles' *Electra* stretch the psyche of the protagonist around an action whose plan is doubly known to the audience, in the myth, and in the explicit deliberation of the prologue between Orestes and the Paidagogus (45–60). The double murder stands patently on the surface, and the plan for it boldly begins the sequence. The justification for the matricide, however, lies profoundly beneath the surface, where it had taken Aeschylus a whole trilogy to justify it, and Euripides brought the Dioscuri in as *dei ex machina* to effectuate the justification.

Sophocles' Electra remains alone through much of the play; the cooperation of Orestes occurs in the irony of the audience's silent knowledge, but the recognition scene is postponed almost to the end of the play (1220–26), an all-but-final tautening for Electra's emotions. And by then she has run the gamut, as Kitto says[7] "of the great human emotions . . . pure grief, weariness, impatience, anger, scorn, contempt, despair, heroic elation, iron determination, unrestrained joy, pitiless hatred." In the *Choephoroi* the recognition takes place early enough (225–35) for brother and sister to work together through most of the play, and in Euripides' *Electra* it occupies a position at the center (575–83). At the center of this play, however, we are given, complete with messenger speech, the false announcement of Orestes' death; and our irony distances us to watch the logic of deployed reactions in Electra herself. Sophocles' alteration of his predecessors' tempo subjects her pathos to the necessity of bearing the events in solitude, of uniting the rejection by her mother, with which Euripides begins, to the purpose of avenging her father. The mighty impact of her brother's supposed death lasts through the long middle of the play (673–1220), producing a dramatic effect upon her which is not as it seems a final term, but a preliminary one, in the proportions of her self-management.

The last words of the chorus describe the transition "from pathos to liberation" which the action of the play has been organized to demonstrate:

> Ὦ σπέρμ' Ἀτρέως, ὡς πολλὰ παθὸν
> δι' ἐλευθερίας μόλις ἐξῆλθες
> τῇ νῦν ὁρμῇ τελεωθέν.

> O seed of Atreus how, suffering much,
> You have barely come through freedom
> And are perfected in this rush.                        (1508–10)

The "rush" (ὁρμῇ) of the action, and the "suffering" (παθόν) of Electra have just managed to carry off a perfection, and the demonstration of this, as Charles Segal uneasily points out,[8] occurs without any sort of justifying statement that Sophocles often gives us, and that both Aeschylus and Euripides give us in this very case. Here Sophocles purifies the action entirely through the patterned responses of Electra herself. Everything depends on that rhythm, which is invested, finally, in the last masterstroke of the presentation: Aegisthus pulls back the cover from the face of the corpse whom he thinks to be the dead Orestes and sees to be the dead Clytemnestra. At that one moment he recapitulates, in reverse, Electra's long trajectory from hopeless sorrow to hopeful joy. At that moment she has already perfected her state by anticipation; she is silent before the stichomathy between Orestes and Aegisthus. Her last words have ironically (1) proffered joy to Aegisthus:

> May you rejoice, if this turns out to be joyful for you    (1457)

and (2) have put the seal on her own sequence:

> And my things are finished. For in time
> I have held my mind so as to bear with the stronger. (1464–65)

To this main movement of the central character, from hopeless sorrow to hopeful joy, all the alternations that Segal notices are subordinated, the biological metaphor embedded in the verb "complete" repeated above, and the frequent contrast, basic to a drama's language about action, between language *(logos)* and action *(ergon)*.[9] As he says, "Sophocles has written a work wherein the action is almost pure emotion, where *logos* (as it is connected with Electra) has the substance of *ergon*"—or the other way around, the *ergon* of the play constitutes its own *logos*, nakedly, without the interposition of justificatory structures. Or as Waldock says "the art of dramatic suppression . . . is the dominant technique."[10] To this plain movement are subordinated all the "interplay between life and death and light and darkness . . . ricochet of the dramatic action . . . in increasingly rapid succession."[11] Electra dominates all this interplay, and struggles through it to the clear stage at the end.

Her first speech (86–120) is a pure lament that finds the emphasis of heavily spondaic anapests, and her rhythm is at once picked up by the chorus, who serve to sympathize while providing "moderation, temperance, and prudence," in the words of Errandonea.[12] She is brought, by regular stages, to a decisiveness with which Orestes has begun the play before her entrance, a decisiveness all the more striking for its declaration in the face of a despair over the supposed death of Orestes. In this even the chorus does not always follow her, as it frankly says before her scorn of Clytemnestra:

> Ὁρῶ μένος πνέουσαν· εἰ δὲ σὺν δίκῃ
> ξύνεστι, τοῦδε φροντίδ᾽ οὐκέτ᾽ εἰσορῶ.

I see her breathing anger. If this is so
With justice, I don't yet see her concern for this.   (610–11)

Electra herself wavers (for example, 616–21), but the justice is established in the contour of her responses. The chorus itself is reduced to mere reaction. Through no action on her part, but merely through a concordant response in difficulties where Chrysothemis is alternately too callous (the death of Agamemnon) and too sentimental (the offerings of Orestes, the murder plan), Electra comes clearly into the "perfection" which is the last word of the play.

Sophocles has confined himself just to that cycle, and just to one person in it. All else may be realized, without being said to follow; it follows just because it has not been said. The enactment has set its own proportions to stand for themselves.


3


The "tremendous modernity" of Greek drama in its time—the phrase is Jaeger's[13]—effects a formal balance, a *harmonia* or *isonomia*, between two strands of discourse, the dialogue and the chorus. These two strands, taken from different dialects, and in different meters, emanate from speakers that differ between themselves. In Sophocles' *Antigone*, the balance between Creon and Antigone, which Hegel emphasized, takes place, as he asserts,[14] just in the dialogue, which itself stands in balance to the other strain of discourse, the chorus.

Hegel attributes "pathos" to the dialogue alone, contrasting this whole dominance with the "consciousness" *(Bewusstsein)* of the chorus, an attribution he makes because the chorus reflects on the action. One could, however, reverse these attributions, placing pathos in the plaintive, emotionally conditioned metrical modes of the chorus and consciousness in the tight, logical antitheses of the iambic dialogue. Hegel's separation between pathos and consciousness is unfortunate because they are not held apart, even dialectically, in the tragedies; the tragedians' triumphant achievement is to fuse pathos and consciousness, point for point, through the proportional sequences in which dialogue and chorus serve as both histrionic and metrical constituents.

In the dialogue, Antigone is fixed against Creon, not just as family against state, Hegel's opposition, or as loving against hating,[15] but ultimately as one who is justified in death against one whom the suicide of son and wife have shown to be unjustifiably wrong, a conclusion it takes the mounting, proportional events of the play to bring about.

Over and above this fixed *agon*, the chorus projects the freedom of their transcendant meditations, again and again. The meter of dialogue is fixed; its associations, through heightened Attic back to Archilochus and Indo-European[16] origins, also remain fixed. But the meter of the choruses is free—it may choose among several modes; it may even, on occasion, choose the iambic itself. Those choices provide options of emotional emphasis (Doric is sterner and simpler than the excited Aeolic, not itself so wrought up as the Paeonic), of geographical association within Greece, and of possible patterning with the meters that go before and after (where iambic can only repeat iambic). The chorus is further free to choose what its role will be towards persons— whether it will voice the protagonist's sentiments, its own, or those of the author, or some combination of these—and it is free in any of these voices to choose its stance to the immediately preceding action.

In the wider swing of its proportions, the chorus of the *Antigone* serves to expand the implications and qualify the mood of the play.

In the parodos of the *Antigone*, the Theban elders turn away from the deadlock between the young sisters and address not the remote past of the family, which Ismene has adduced, but the immediate past of the fight in which Polyneices has acted and over whose corpse they are arguing.

αἰετὸς εἰς γῆν ὣς ὑπερέπτα,
λευκῆς χιόνος πτέρυγι στεγανός

as an eagle flying over the land,
covering himself with a wing of white snow     (113–14)

Their chant of joy at the salvation of Thebes drowns in this image of
magnificence the sense that Polyneices is hostile. They have begun
with an invocation to the sun, in a long, Aeolic line that proclaims this
light to be the best, cutting back to shorter glyconics for completion,
and swinging on out into a majestic statement that, when it does get
to naming Polyneices, reverts to martial anapests, or something that
echoes them (110–16). The exact metrical correspondences of strophe
to antistrophe, and here also of *systema* to *systema*, counter the even,
forward progression of the iambic dialogue with a kind of circular
movement that the dance and the melody would further have emphasized. One line is far freer to vary than the fixed iamb. But a series
of lines recurs in colametric patterning.

The choral account of the victory also repeats. The awe over
Polyneices that here masters the hostility towards him, renders
inextricable already, in the joy of the chorus, the two positions that
Ismene and Antigone have taken respectively, and also the one that
Creon will shortly take. It ends the account of Zeus' action against the
proud besiegers by linking the two brothers in their end, "they got
both of them the share of a common death" (146–47).

Before looking out to announce the arrival of Creon in the last set of
anapests[17] it asks, in its song and dance, for a song and dance of victory
celebration to bring "forgetfulness of the present things" (151–52).
In the concluding Adonean, of this second antistrophe's short cap to
the long sweep of the penultimate Aeolic line, it asks that the leader of
the dance be "Bacchic" (154)! Thus it gives the name of Dionysus, the
tutelary god of Thebes, as well as of the dramatic festival, to the mood
it has been invoking, a pause of complete, formal resolution to the war
by asserting the connection between this special group of men (Theban
elders are speaking) and their gods, Zeus and Dionysus. This resolution
is shattered rhythmically by the swelling iambs of Creon's immediately
ensuing proclamation; it is shattered logically by what he proclaims,

that Polyneices is to be singled out, contradicting their assertion, and not to be buried.

After this first episode, which locks on the interchange of threat and terror between Creon and the herald who has announced the forbidden burial, the chorus commences its first *stasimon* with two sweeping Aeolic lines of Glyconics in *synartete* with a type of Aeolic dimeter.[18] A long line strengthens the modal assertiveness of a measure, and the two long lines hold the assertiveness even more than the single long line with which the *parodos* opened. Here the threat and terror find a name in the adjective δεινός, terrible and awesome.

This second chorus now chooses to refer specifically to the event immediately preceding, as Gerhart Müller points out.[19] However, its main reference is not the passing implication of the brazen burial, but rather a conspectus of man himself as δεινός in all his activities:

> πολλὰ τὰ δεινὰ κοὐδὲν ἀνθρώπου δεινότερον πέλει
> τοῦτο καὶ πολιοῦ πέραν πόντου χειμερίῳ νότῳ
> χωρεῖ, περιβρυχίοισιν
> περῶν ὑπ᾽ οἴδμασιν,
> θεῶν τε τὰν ὑπερτάταν, Γᾶν
> ἄφθιτον ἀκαμάταν, ἀποτρύεται
> ἰλλομένων ἀρότρων ἔτος εἰς ἔτος,
> ἱππείῳ γένει πολεύων.

Many awesome things there are, yet nothing exists more
    awesome than man.
Thus does he go even beyond the hoary ocean in the wintry
    south wind,
Crossing under the swells troughing round.
And the highest of gods, the Earth,
Undying, unperishing, does he wear away,
By his turning plow year after year
With the horse-brood digging it up . . .                    (332–40)

At once the elders are invoking a vision that goes far beyond the play in one sense, and yet in another sense this chorus handles the pressing moral problems by an ambiguous transcendence; the activities it lists at its pitch offer only the suggestion of metaphor for the locked concerns of the play.

Their mood takes us not to the depths of Creon's confrontation with Antigone but away from them in a serenity that undermines him (he has been the immediately preceding contraversialist; their vision counteracts his obsession) but only questions her (in what sense is the deed which later turns out to be hers an awesome one?), a question somewhat deflected by the fact that Creon is looking for a male culprit and the chorus naturally uses the masculine for the generically human —though to be sure, as Knox points out,[20] the sexes are switched later on; the masculinity of Antigone, which makes her either heroic or unnatural (both are senses of δεινός), may be included by distant implication in these utterances.

The freedom of the chorus here elaborately exemplifies the Sophoclean principle that Walter Jens[21] formulates, that the references tend to be both immediate and distant: "Die Hintergründigkeit des sophokleischen Dramas liegt in der Doppeldeutigkeit der Worte, die zugleich vordergründig-situationsbezogen and hintergründig-endbezogen sind." Their long, general utterance supersedes the myopic tyranny of Creon, providing thus early a kind of long-range confidence into which Antigone's defense of the proper law between man and god may find its proper perspective among the awesomeness of man's achievements— but not yet, and not explicitly. Creon's threat and the craven collaboration of the Herald on the one side; on the other side, this contemplation of the arts of peace, which stands in balance not just to the dialogue, but to the victory ode of the *parodos*, much as the peace similes in the *Iliad* balance the war scenes. Kranz sees something Sophistic in the sharpness of this ode's distinctions.[22] But its effect is not argumentative; it provides a larger background for the conflict, just as the background of current Athenian law (traitors are not buried, ties by marriage prevail over blood ties)[23] remains a background for Antigone's problem, which happens to deny the first law and equivocate in the second.

Choral poetry is an enchanted ground; the invocation of an awesomeness in human agriculture and sailing, language and statesmanship, has carried the chorus further than it wanted to go at the beginning, something that is not really possible in dialogue. By the end it is clear that its explicit intention has been merely to condemn the breaker of the edict, in an antithesis:

νόμους παρείρων χθονὸς θεῶν τ᾽ ἔνορκον δίκαν
ὑψίπολις· ἄπολις ὅτῳ τὸ μὴ καλὸν
ξύνεστι τόλμας χάριν.

Who weaves in the laws and the sworn justice of earth and
the gods
Is high in the city; without a city is he with whom
What is not good abides, because of his daring     (369–71)

ὑψίπολις-ἄπολις—"high in the city–cityless"—is climactic in this great ode. The terms center on that sense of community where the human law converges with the divine, and where the "distributive management," which is one of the meanings of the verb behind νόμους, finds an embodiment not only abstract but concretely visible in the ranged audience at the theater. The whole city went, and those with whom this imperial city was associated, visitors from over the seas newly navigable in the spring. Anyone who did not have a ticket was provided one by the city, to be part of the city.

*Nomos* is opposed to *phusis*—or, as we would say, culture opposed to nature—in the writings of Plato. But *nomos* and *physis* are linked in the assumptions of the tragedians, implicity and even sometimes explicitly (*Eur.* Frag. 168, *Cyclops* 649, Frag. 904; but *contra*, Frag. 1113, *Soph. OC* 337–38).

*Polis* comprises the values that are embodied in the *Antigone*, since she as well as Creon asserts the civic virtues. The word itself occurs thirty-seven times in that one play (three more if we count *politai*, citizens), as it does abundantly in the tragedians. But the value in tragedy is too substantive, and the adjectival form *politikos*, already in current use by Herodotus and Thucydides among others, does not occur a single time in the whole of tragic literature.

"The person without a city" in the antithetic attribution of the ode, the ἄπολις, will turn out to be Creon, and not Antigone. At the moment, the chorus seems to mean that Creon is "high in the city," and the

Man who "taught city-law passions" (ἀστυνόμους ὀργὰς ἐδιδάξατο,
355) is clearly acting as Creon acted in the governing declarations
of his entrance (165–74). Still, "passions" (ὀργὰς) has a prevailingly
evil sense in Greek, and that evil sense has not long to sleep (see 436)
as the ὀργή of Creon's action comes clear.

The ὑψίπολις–ἄπολις antithesis echoes another in the ode, the
preceding παντοπόρος–ἄπορος, "All-coping, non-coping," (360) which
comes in the same line and the same position of the preceding strophe,
itself echoing the περιφραδὴς ("universal-minded," 347) in the same
position of the preceding antistrophe. While formally an antithesis,
ἄπορος, in its meaning merely asserts the capability that the other two
assert: "he is non-coping for nothing that is to be" (παντοπόρος· ἄπορος
ἐπ' οὐδὲν ἔρχεται 360). The double negative, however, turns out to
be ominous for Creon, and ominous in a different sense—though
finally upheld—for Antigone.

The chorus is aiming its language at damning a culprit, and after
the formal strophic pattern has been fulfilled, it rides over into anapest
echoes again, naming Antigone who has just been brought in by the
guard. That action joins the coming second episode with the prior first
episode, with the guard's last terrified speech. By exonerating him,
the chorus closes the trap of dialogue once more, after opening it to
the heavens.

Antigone, who was shown urging principle on her sister in the prologue;
and Creon, who was shown forcing an edict on a subordinate in the
first episode; now come together in this second episode to argue
the basis of the human law that has been praised as an awesome
achievement in the choral eulogy. The δεινά of the great chorus comes
up in the herald's speech (407); hybris enters Creon's accusation (480,
482, ὑπέρ in 481); the laws enter the discussions of both (νόμους, 449,
452, 481, 519). The episode ends with the imprisonment of both sisters,
and the chorus moves into a second stasimon in a more subdued hexa-
podic line of the same number of feet as the iambic trimeter, beginning
in the loose dactylo-epitrites[24] and lapsing at once into the iambs that
echo and exemplify the dominance of the dialogue.

This stasimon is downed by the action and merely bemoans the fate
of those whose "house is shaken by the god" (584), a determinism
counterbalancing, and momentarily canceling, the awesome sense

of human achievement in the first *stasimon*. Now man does not ride over the sea swell; rather, he explicitly resembles it (586–91). So far, the first strophe and antistrophe. The second strophe and antistrophe revive the Aeolic measures of the first two odes; they now praise the gods in language reminiscent of the praise for man in the first *stasimon*:

> τεάν, Ζεῦ, δύνασιν τίς ἀνδρῶν ὑπερβασία κατάσχοι
> τὰν οὔθ' ὕπνος αἱρεῖ ποθ' ὁ πάντ' ἀγεύρων,
> οὔτε θεῶν ακματοι μῆνες 'αγῆρως δὲ χρόνῳ
> δυνάστας κατέχεις 'Ολύμπου μαρμαρόεσσαν αἴγλαν.
> τό τ' ἔπειτα καὶ τὸ μέλλον
> καὶ τὸ πρὶν ἐπαρκέσει
> νόμος ὅδ', οὐδὲν ἕρπει
> θνατῶν βιότῳ πάμπολις ἐκτὸς ἄτας.

What excess of men could constrain your power, Zeus?
Which sleep, the all-catching, never snares?
Nor the tireless moons of the gods, but ageless in time
You hold as a ruler Olympus's shining gleam.
> For the then and the coming
> And the before there suffices
> This law. Nothing creeps
> All whole for the life of mortals without ruination. (604–14)

The word *ate* occurs twice more before the end of the *stasimon*, and while it has seemed, when the meter changed, to be reversing the hope-despair of the sequence in the first *stasimon*; it now ends, as that one did, on a confrontation of despair.

These three odes, taken together, offer a progressive tightening of the perspective, or darkening of the atmosphere. The marvellous invocation of the first, the visionary scope of the second, serve to intensify the tightening, as well as to qualify it by being the only places in the play where the emotional effect of realized justice can find anticipatory expression. This tightening had happened in the face of Antigone's assertions of love in the second episode. The third episode, in which Haimon stands on his love for Antigone and Creon pronounces he will entomb her where she can "honor Hades" (777), is followed by a third *stasimon* that sings the invincibility of Eros.

This fourth ode, the longest so far, alternates with lyric utterances by the condemned Antigone herself. (This dialogue is listed by conventional analysis as a separate *kommos*, but it is dramatically and metrically continuous with the prevailing glyconics or glyconic echoes of the Aeolic third *stasimon*.) Love brings the men of the first *stasimon* and the gods of the second together; first because that god is irresistible to men, and next because the other gods, like men, also find him irresistible (783–90). As lauding the principle of Haimon, the ode looks back. But it also looks ahead; it warns as well as praises: Eros is dangerous. When Antigone appears, the images of love will be variously combined with images of death, anticipating in lyric form the offstage dramatic result of double death for the entombed lovers. They answer her long Aeolic lines, which echo their own prior ones, with short anapests that thereby vary their own utterances and also hers. They interrupt the images, and the exemplum of Niobe, offering one consolatory set of abstractions:

> But she was a god and born of gods,
> And we are mortals and mortal-born.
> Yet for one who dies it is great to be said
> To have shared a lot equal with gods
> When living, and then when dying.          (834–38)

The lyric accessibility of the chorus has enabled it to cast its habitual platitudes in a form that does justice to Antigone's justice, transcending even the Eros that had begun to be their focus.

They end, though, by condemning her, while she ends by bemoaning her descent, and her solitary, unwed state, as much as the fact of her death. In the ensuing fourth episode, as Creon mocks her, she goes to pieces, exhibiting in the negation of dialogue what she had lamented positively in the choral strophes: she would not have sacrificed herself for husband or offspring as she would for a brother, because a brother alone is irreplaceable (905–15). She thus projects the condition of being "deserted, bereft" (ἔρημος, 919) onto the object of her piety and the cause of her death, and, in assertion only, cutting herself off from the lover who waits her in the underground tomb.

The leap from the tense logic of her argument in the second episode to the dream-like extremes of these final utterances is prepared for as a possibility by the leaps and fusions of the odes chanted by the much more limited elders. Here she shows herself to be the woman whom the devotion of Haimon and the ode to Eros call up. The condemnation has taken its psychological toll first on her, before it destroys the family of Creon; and then on Creon himself. Lapsing into anapests, she simply indicates herself in her last words as the last of her line, suffering for piety (μούνην λοιπήν . . . πάσχω, τὴν εὐσεβίαν σεβίσασα, 941–43).

In the shorter Aeolic measures of their fourth *stasimon*, the chorus now takes refuge wholly in three examples of imprisoned people, expanding the form of the Niobe theme in the previous ode. The first example, Danae, may be taken as complimentary to Antigone; but the second, that of a Lycurgus who was punished for flouting the Dionysus they have already invoked, cannot be taken so; except that he is a man, and may be referred ahead to Creon also. Cleopatra, the third example, is imprisoned with her children. She has descendants as Antigone does not; but they, like her, have none; and they were blinded (973–75), as Ismene has mentioned that Oedipus was (52–53). Among these implicit correspondences is an analogy to the Creon who is shortly to lose the second of his two sons, as well as his wife.

Creon is immediately warned, in the ensuing fifth episode, by a character new to the play but not to the legend, Tiresias. The prophet's injunction to bury Polyneices so as to ward off pollution from the state, repeats Antigone's to Ismene in the prologue.

Creon capitulates at once. The chorus responds to this denouement, not with another *stasimon* but with a *hyporchema*, one long, simple Aeolic invocation to Bacchus that he save them from the difficulty. This new simplicity carries its own omen, in the face of the complex counter-balances between dialogue and ode that have gone before.

At once, in the sixth episode, dialogue serves only the purpose of a brief announcement and fatal incitement: at a messenger's report of Haimon's death, another new character, Creon's wife, Eurydice, withdraws to kill herself.

The dochmiacs of intense emotion have mainly been reserved for the final song, where the chorus shares the repartee of sorrow with the broken Creon. In its epilogue, it leaves the dochmiacs for a mixture of choriambs and anapests. It closes by asserting that old age teaches wisdom, a maxim its own responses can be said to exemplify only if these responses are set in the whole ordered alternation between chorus and dialogue I have been tracing.

The higher law to which Antigone has done homage finds its abstract statement in the case she makes during the second episode; it finds its dramatic embodiment in the rhythmic enactment of the proportioned verse, where the vision of a part, and the wide swing from one part to another, testifies to a supreme value in her love, as well as in her piety, a value surviving her suicide as well as her death. In the play the *nomoi* of choral rhythms, set against the even rhythm of dialogue, produce the highest contour, the *rhythmos* for the *nomoi* she herself cannot formulate as well as they do for her. The laws of the play, *nomoi* in both senses, become her law. The *nomos* outlasts the *ate*, within this play's action. In other plays, too, the very proportions, the *isonomia*, of disposed event, constrain the evoked *ate* from evoking naked terror. And Greek plays, by their composedness, all show some *isonomia*. Even the *Hecuba*, in its time-balance, is as Olympian as the *Antigone; nomos* prevails.

# Chapter Six: THEOS

## 1

*Theos* does not mean "god" we are correctly cautioned; but *theos* also does mean god. What is at issue here is no mere problem of translation when meanings partially overlap, but an indeterminability about the gods, one which functions dynamically within Greek tragedy. The scepticism of Xenophanes and others about the gods long precedes tragedy; even Heraclitus' enigmatic remark, "character is a man's leading-spirit," ἦθος ἀνθρώπῳ δαίμων,[1] where *daimon* means "a not-yet-ascertained god," may be seen in an atheistic light: "no mysterious other force is a man's leading spirit," he seems to be saying, "but his own habitual bent." "The fault, dear Brutus, lies not in our stars, but in ourselves." In this light his mysterious aphorism "mortals are immortal and immortals mortal, living their own death, dying their own life,"[2] which can be given a mystic meaning, can also be taken to erase a distinction that had been carefully maintained in the language.

Death is the very point—and especially so in a dramatic form concerned with both death and the gods—at which the notions of mortal man and the immortal gods do meet, first by the contradiction inherent in the contrast, but next by the sort of transformation which an Alcestis, a Hippolytus, an Oedipus, may undergo, becoming something like gods after passing through death. In the tragedies, heroes like Theseus and Heracles are often seen resolving questions of death, or visiting the underworld. Heracles especially is variously associated with death in the *Alcestis*, *The Children of Heracles*, *The Madness of Heracles*, the *Trachiniai*, the *Hippolytus*, and perhaps (coming long after the death of Io) the *Prometheus Bound* among the extant plays; as well as in the lost *Heracleidai* of Aeschylus and the *Heracles* of Sophocles, in addition to the *Auge*, the *Perithous*, and perhaps the *Eurystheus* of Euripides.

Death as a point of contact between man and god may produce complications as well as confusions. The *Hippolytus*, on one axis, offers mortal men of two kinds, plain ones like the nurse and those of semi-divine descent like Hippolytus and Phaedra; it also offers heroes like Theseus and the Heracles he has been helping; and gods like Aphrodite and Artemis. On another axis the distinction between life and death, applicable to men only, stands at the beck of the Theseus who in the myth may go with impunity to the underworld and call on Poseidon to kill his son; and the son may cross over the distinction by becoming a cult-figure, while at the same time irrevocably and pitiably dying in his human form.

The Dionysiac ritual carries, through its sacrifices and its central figure, reminiscences of the dying god (a mortal immortal). In specific plays there are traces, sometimes explicit, of some identification between the dead and the divine, as in the *Alcestis* (1002–3, 1015), when it is said the sacrificed wife will be invoked as a god after her death; or the *Choephoroi*, where Orestes and Electra pray with the chorus to Agamemnon almost as though he had divine powers. Athene herself in the *Eumenides* links the immortals and the dead when describing the power of the Furies: (a power which is to be "dim-eyed," ἀμβλωπόν, among men):

> The queenly Fury has
> Great power over the immortals
> And with those under the earth.         (950–52)

So pervasive is the tendency in tragedy to blur, or at least not to invoke, the distinction between men and gods, that in spite of a central concern for both death and the gods, the common word *athanatos*, "non-dying, god," appears only five times in Aeschylus, three times in Sophocles, and twelve times in Euripides; and prevailingly in an adjectival use of some other quality, occurring only twice, once, and twice, respectively, as a substantive.

What Kitto says of the first extant tragedy, the *Persians*[3] may, *mutatis mutandis*, be said of all: "No sharp line is drawn between humanity and inanimate nature. Both move in a certain regular pattern, and the pattern reveals, or is expressed by, the gods. So the double plane . . .

is the traditional poetic Greek way of indicating the universal pattern
to which the particular event conforms."

Altars stood before the stage, and sometimes on stage. Any set of
conventions—familial piety, political loyalty, marital fidelity, reverence for the dead—carries with it, for stage group and audience
group, a stable relation to the gods, just as the special relation with
Aphrodite or Lussa may create an unstable and catastrophic one. The
very birds, so often mentioned in the choruses of Euripides and elsewhere, even when not used for divination, carry with them reminiscences of a mana widespread in ancient Hellenic culture.[4] The action
in many plays starts from some special position of a god—as do, for
example, the *Prometheus*, the *Hippolytus*, the *Ajax*, and the *Trojan
Women*—or from some special divine utterance, an oracle.

In Euripides all the action of a play is often referred to the gods
under the principle that "many are the forms of the daimonic." The
*deus ex machina* itself, then, as well as constituting the incursion of a
being from a different plane of existence, also illustrates the principle,
standing as an event climatic but charged like any other, one among
the many "unexpected things" (ἄελπτά) that the gods achieve. Medea,
who is of semidivine origin, transposes her ferocity of monstrous self-
justification by arriving in a chariot to serve as her own *deus ex machina*.

If the forms of the demonic are many, then they are subjected to
chance, to *tuche*, a common word in Euripides. But the *deux ex machina*,
a chance event in itself, breaks the pattern of other chances by standing
for the dominance of the appearing god. In the chariot that her divine
ancestor has provided, Medea is psychologically as well as physically
removed from the interactions of the drama.

The gods come perilously close to abstractions, Aphrodite as erotic
power, Dionysus as a union of creative force and death; or sometimes
the abstractions are gods, Ananke and Lussa and Eros. The god combines the deified abstractions in this fragment from the *Andromeda*:[5]

> They say that Justice is the child of Zeus,
> And dwells close to the error of mortal men,

This notion links the *hamartia* Aristotle finds in tragedy generally with its defining balance-scale, Justice, and Justice with a source in a divine personage.

## 2

Bringing the gods into the light of enactment raises not just the abstract philosophical questions that were discussed and applied at the time. By activating an emotional sequence of events across the orchestra to the elevated silence of the audience, the tragic enactment must have released for poetic consideration a general current of feeling toward the gods; that is, toward the inexplicable forces that govern events. Tragedy must have done so because in its wide and coherent frame it resurrects, and therefore actively engages, forces that had been conventionalized since Homer. It is often said that Aeschylus is more primitive than Homer, and on the contrary that Euripides is archly skeptical towards the gods. But the question of human sacrifice, not as a given but as a dynamic element combinatory with other dramatic elements, already vestigial in Homer, is scarcely to be found in Aeschylus, while in one form or another it pervades many of Euripides' plays.

Tragedy, enacted within a framework where animal sacrifices precede the performance, carries, to begin with, reminiscences of sacrifice, the sacrifice of a man or of an animal substituted for him. Moreover, in the sense that the audience is purged by going through the representation of the sufferings on stage, every tragedy symbolically reproduces a sacrificial pattern. In plays like *Prometheus Bound, Oedipus Rex,* and *The Bacchae,* the pattern is not blurred but sharp: one figure suffers extraordinarily in ways for which the gods are responsible, and each play dwells on the mystery of that responsibility. Here the symbolic sacrifice is presented for the contemplation of the audience, and if it is to apprehend the sense of it, to be "gripped," it must attend to both the difference (*eleos*, pity) and the likeness (*phobos*, terror) of the Aristotelian catharsis. Its responses cannot be assimilated, again, to the rejection of likeness through the assertion of difference between them, even by setting up a dialectic. This is what Girard[6] reads into tragedy, and into literature generally, by pointing out, in the process of discovering it at a new level of profundity, the connection between all human "desire" and the pattern of sacrifice as a one-way "offering" to the gods. Nor can the subsequent reaction of the audience be considered a "rejection" of the identity-horror in sacrifice. The spectator must be conceived of as "remembering" and not as "forgetting" the play (or otherwise any horror story would do the same work; there would be no special character to Sophocles); nor can the literary contemplation of sacrificial patterns be considered a substitution for the real performance thereof, since human sacrifice, in the particular form that Euripides revives it within his imagined scene, had probably been gone for centuries, anyway, from the actual scene of Greek life.

To be sure, the riddling presence of sacrifice as some aspect of the imagined scene is attenuated in the *Alcestis*, where we have a substitution rather than a sacrifice proper; in the *Hippolytus*, where the revenge-death is transfigured after the fact rather than before; in the *Ajax*, which begins with a substitute slaughter of animals, improper because *non-sacrificial*, and ends by consistently deploring the hero's suicide; in the *Trachiniai*, where the funeral pyre in its sacrificial setting is given no sacrificial relation to the events; in the *Antigone*, where the heroine is sent underground, under conditions reminiscent of sacrifice, because she has violated a civil ordinance that is still operative[7] in the actual scene of contemporary Athens; in the *Oedipus at Colonus*, where Oedipus, who has survived one sacrificial matrix, does hallow Athens by his death but disappears mysteriously in the depths of a grove.

In Euripides the sacrifice is often explicit, or nearly so. The killing of Neoptolemos in the *Andromache* is something like a sacrifice, as the "sacrifice" of Polyxena in the *Trojan Women* and the *Hecuba* is something like a murder. Evadne's self-immolation in the *Suppliants* resembles, in its resoluteness and in its sudden, discontinous appearance, the voluntary sacrifices of Macaria in the *Children of Heracles* and Menoeceus in the *Phoenissai*.

In other plays the explicit sacrifice becomes problematical: one of Euripides' last plays, the *Iphigenia at Aulis*, focuses every major personage on the Greek side of the Trojan War upon the question of whether or not Iphigenia should be sacrificed, and the unresolvable question is finally solved by a divine intervention, the substitution of an animal for the victim.

In a long speech preserved from the lost *Erechtheus*,[8] that king justifies the sacrifice of his daughter to win a war, on the basis of duty to the *polis*. By setting an admitted civic principle in the light of an actual practice inadmissible to his audience—and Erechtheus stresses the necessity of *erga*, deeds, not just *logoi*, words (13)—and by relating both sacrifice and civic duty to the problematical practice of receiving problematical oracles, Euripides is invoking a modality for which the name irony would be too simple, since at no point, presumably, did the play imply direct blame for the praised event. Yet its undeniable blameworthiness is caught up into relation with other values, just as the principle of military expediency, urgent in the Peloponnesian War, is given the guise of cruelty in the *Hecuba* and the *Trojan Women*. One cannot, however, ascribe utter pacifistic cynicism to the demonstrably patriotic Euripides.

A comparable inadmissibility provides an ironic center for the *Iphigenia in Tauris*, where the rescued but captive victim-turned-priestess is reduced to accepting the practice that all Greeks may be sacrificed at the barbarian altar; she is all the more willing to plunge into this cruelty as an escape from the news of her brother Orestes' death. He himself links the murder of his mother to the fact that he will be sacrificed:

Having killed my mother, I will be destroyed myself. (715)

After Iphigenia deludes the Taurian king Thoas so as to escape with Orestes and Pylades, the three are caught, and Thoas will confound sacrifice with murder by killing them. He is stopped by Athene, who institutes a festival of sacrifice that floods the end of the play in altered significance. This sacrifice is metonymic, as it were, since it consists of blood taken by a sword from a man's throat (1459–61), a ritual connected with the rule of tie-breaking acquittal on the Areopagus (1470–73). The play's return to Athens through the person of Athene, and the incursion of the etiological myth—the *deus ex machina* and the symbolic sacrifice—are not self-explanatory because they merely cap the other human disturbances, where the blood-guilt and family justification of Orestes are deployed against an apposition between barbarian and Greek through the means, and also toward the end, of an unacceptable but insistent primitive management of the gods.

3

In Euripides what is tragicomic in the emotional dimension becomes an enigmatic modality in the dimension of the gods' acts toward men. When he treats a legend, there is a pronounced tendency, on the other hand, toward the explicit in the form of completeness: the *Iphigenia at Aulis* offers both a special angle on the figures of the Trojan War and a survey of those figures, as the *Andromache*, the *Hecuba*, the *Trojan Women*, and in its own way the *Helen*, provide a complete view of war's aftermath, any war through the lens of this war. The *Orestes* orders an entire community around the question of how to handle the guilty survivors of a family curse, and the *Phoenissai*, if it were completely successful, would be a diorama of the Theban legend.

Over the foreground action, however complete, the gods stand in wait, moving and shining powerfully behind their veil. Dolon in the *Rhesus* speaks of:

ψυχὴν προβάλλοντ' ἐν κύβοισι δαίμονος.

Casting the soul forth on the dice of the god     (183)

a statement whose periphrasis of *tuche* exists in ironic perspective towards the audience generally, since in the well-known episode from the *Iliad* he himself gets killed; the die is already cast. His statement also presents an irony towards the sequence of this particular play, since he exemplifies far too simple a view of military action, of feinting, hostility and the like; the truth of his maxim covers a situation too simple for his fate and also too complex for his utterance of the maxim. The veil is not pulled aside.

The *Helen* puts the whole Trojan War at one remove from the veil; it has been fought over a phantom Helen. Euripides takes the alternate legend delineated by Stesichorus, combines it with the extreme rhetorical stance of Gorgias' *Defense of Helen*, and makes his audience wonder, not about Helen but about the gods: she has been put there by a Hera jealous over the judgment of Paris while the real Helen has been kept safe, and innocent, in Egypt. The events of the war are canvassed in Helen's dialogue with Teucer (75–166) in the light of identifying her and Menelaus. If the play touched at all seriously on the war, it would collapse under the bitterness about so much suffering over a mere mistaken identity, of human impotence before the gods. As it is, the outcome of the war for Menelaus is to fit him to become a semidivine being through his toils ($\pi\acute{o}\nu o\iota$, 1679), which have a re-demptive value in themselves, regardless of the dubiousness of their cause. In the arch complications of the error, Menelaus, least heroic of the Greeks, is put through the paces of a situation that would try an Odysseus.

The audience begins with the truth of this error; Helen announces the story in her prologue. Our irony, then holds everyone, and as Zuntz points out[9] "everyone of the persons of the play is seen on the way from error to truth." And further, "this irony gives the play its lightness and verve as well as its profundity; it connects, dissociates, mingles gods and men." Even so, the true beauty of Helen has truly caused the war; so she herself says:

> My gifts
> From Kypris bore much blood,
> Much of tears . . .                                    (363–65)

Even before Helen introduces herself in the prologue, however, she tells about the prophetess Theonoe, daughter of the shifting god, Proteus (10–15). Theonoe, at the point where she discovers Menelaus, declares, when at once recognizing the Greek through his incognito (874), that since she knows there is a quarrel in heaven between Hera and Kypris about whether to save them or not, the disposition be-tween those two gods is in her hands. Paradoxically, though, this will be resolved through a mere act of human agency; it depends on whether or not she reveals Menelaus' identity to her brother Theo-cylmenos (Called-God; so Theonoe is God-Thought), who hopes to marry Helen. Her decision not to do so, a simple moral act on the single plane of human behaviour, gets subjected by its inclusion in the sphere of her prophecy to the same questioning modality about the gods. Sentimental events stand in the foreground—a husband rejoins his lost wife; after a close call that leads them to prepare a suicide pact (837) they sail off together. They are shadowed by the mighty background of the purposes of the gods and the intentions of this singular god-descended supernaturally empowered figure. Theonoe herself gets drawn in fatally; her brother will kill her for her deception after the escape; but she is rescued by the Dioscuri, in the *deus ex machina* that announces the apotheosis of Helen and the near apotheosis of Menelaus. The sentiment, itself tragicomic, is plumbed for more than it will bear, after it has been produced by deflating the gigantic legend of the Trojan War. On the other hand, and discordantly, the war's tragedies remain the same. Yet the rhythm touches on the irony; the last line of the chorus that tells of her terrible effects is in *ithyphallic* meter:

> τὸ δ' ἐμὸν δέμας
> ὤλεσεν ὤλεσε πέργαμα Δαρδανίας
> ὀλομένους τ' Ἀχαιούς.

My body
Ruined, ruined the towers of Troy
And the ruined Achaeans      (383–85)

The meter, like the plot, exponentializes the function of the war in the play's view of the gods. The play closes, enigmatically, with the old Euripidean refrain, "Many are the forms of demonic things . . . . " (1688–92).

Here the natural events interact with the irony of demonic providence. When Theoclymenos asks (1186 ff.) why Helen has changed her clothes from white to black, and why she is crying, he has trapped the couple, and yet we know she will escape. The change from white to black is religious, and yet it subverts religion with duplicity, as it cloaks religion over a dazzling beauty that carries all before it (except that the beauty itself has a religious source; it is the gift of the gods). Her tears express her situation, though not to him; they are tears of a mourning that is false, of an anxiety that is true, though itself false in the light of her final escape. Helen is helpless in these complexities, a fact that the tears (behind the mask of the actor), being merely named and not visible, may be taken to express. They are an emotional equivalent of the bewilderment her handmaidens express in the immediately preceding chorus:

ὅ τι θεὸς ἢ μὴ θεὸς ἢ τὸ μέσον,
τίς φησ' ἐρευνήσας βροτῶν
μακρότατον πέρας εὑρεῖν,
ὃς τὰ θεῶν ἐσορᾷ
δεῦρο καὶ αὖθις ἐκεῖσε
καὶ πάλιν ἀντιλόγοις
πηδῶντ' ἀνελπίστοις τύχαις;

What is the god, or not god, or in between,
Who of mortals says he has tracked
And found to the longest bound,
Who sees the things of the gods
Hither and again thither
And back again leaping in contradictory
Unexpected chances?                                         (1137–43)

The causality in this universe never occurs simply within men, or
simply in the realm of the gods beyond; it shuttles, and suspends while
it shuttles, the possibility of their complicities.

The resolving Dioscuri themselves have an ambiguous divine
existence; they "die and do not die" (τεθνᾶσι κοὐ τεθνᾶσι, 138). Helen,
absolved of guilt, protected, in effect, both by Kypris and her enemy
Hera, as well as by Proteus, needs all her human resources to effectuate
her rescue. The sacrifice of a bull in the departing ship, as the blood
pours into the water (1587–88), mingles with a natural combat against
the pursuing barbarians, the human act substantiating the divine at
this anxious point. The cause blurs here, though it is clearly to be
located again in the silence of Theonoe, itself to be derived from her
special relation to the gods. The chorus just before the escape, while
Helen is still uncertain of the outcome, strangely rises to praise the
Great Mother Demeter (1301–68), a goddess who seems totally un-
related, except that the functions of Hera (power) and Aphrodite (love)
are attributed to her generally, and specifically through two further
figures who are adduced for power and love, Athene (1316) and
Artemis (1315). Zeus enters this ode if Hera does not (1317, 1337–40),
and Kypris plays a tight-stretched tympanum to the accompaniment
of Demeter's flute (1348–52)! All these gods are brought to bear on

Helen, who meanwhile, discordantly and ironically, has been preparing Menelaus's cenotaphic funeral rites.

In asking of her fate (255), Helen early balances alternatives:

> A portent is my life and my affairs,
> These through Hera, but beauty is the cause.  (260–61)

"Daughter," the messenger says to a Helen momentarily silent before her newly discovered husband, "the god is by nature subtle / and hard to evidence (ὁ θεὸς ὡς ἔφυ τι ποικίλον καὶ δυστέκμαρτον, 711–12). Theonoe, who burns her ritual flame to the *aether* (866) but also to the gods generally (871), brings in a declaration that leaves mortal men, though somehow differently, in the same ambiguous status as the Dioscuri:

> There is a payment of these things for those below
> And for all men who are above. The mind
> Of the dead does not live, but it has a thought
> Undying, falling into undying aether.       (1013–16)

The god is a natural act, a natural act is the gods: so Helen says

> O gods! For it is a god to know your friends       (560)

"There is nothing more useful for mortals," the final messenger says, "than prudent mistrust" (1617–18), and the maxim, here a natural one, echoes with the modality that suspends the gods here between mistrust and trust, as it suspends men between ignorant helplessness and visionary capability.

### 4

The riddling presence of a god permeates the *Ion*, of the Apollo at whose shrine the play takes place. He ambiguously dominates the past of Creusa, on whom he once has fathered the Ion now serving his altar, and who has come to Delphi to seek an oracle about her childlessness. Since the oracle he gives seems to declare her husband Xuthus as the father of Ion, Apollo comes through to men under a cloud of falsity, just as he had acted on Creusa in a way that shocks her son. At the same time Ion is overpietistic, and no clear moral definition of the past can be formulated either from his simple reactions or from the possibly self-imposed sufferings of Creusa.

Nor can falsity be imputed to the oracle, a question that bothers Ion even after he has learned his true parentage (1537). The prediction of Hermes (67–73) may mislead in this respect, as it does about whether Creusa's union with the god is kept secret.

To Ion's question about the oracle, "Born from you or the gift of others," (σὸν γεγῶτ' ἤ δῶρον ἄλλων, 537), Xuthus replies contradictorily, "A gift, yet sprung from me" (δῶρον, ὄντα δ'ἐξ ἐμοῦ). And to the question of female parentage he says " I was so pleased at the first, I didn't ask that" (τερφθείς τοῦτο, κεῖν' οὐκ ἠρόμην, 541). The oracle, then, enters the plane we see of human action only through possible distortion; no certain falsehood is ascribed to Apollo. Ion's easy belief of Xuthus' interpretation (he calls him "father," 633, 781, and goes off to a banquet celebrating the parentage) does not alter the dimension of possibility. As for the facts, we know them from Hermes' account in the prologue, which influences nothing, but merely sets the stage for folly.

Apollo is kept carefully offstage, though Athene comes in as a *deus ex machina*. His oracle, since it is not quoted, is not wholly absolved of having been shaped so as to mislead Xuthus. The epithet *Loxias*, "oblique," is the god's most frequent designation in the play. Moreover, oracles, to the Greeks, were notoriously framed in a misleading fashion, a fact which might have given Xuthus pause, or over which the play seems to be pausing.

On the other hand, if oracles are questionable, portents are not; the dove that lands on Ion's poisoned cup (1199–1200) saves his life. Nor is there any evidence in the play for presuming with Verrall[10] that he is not really the child of the god.

The changes in the play can all be attributed to a human folly gone unpredictable under the pressure of the sentiment enacted before our eyes. The orphan is delighted to find a father; the barren woman is beside herself to be told she will never have another child. Creusa is willing to plan the death of Xuthus and Ion; her son, in shocked response, is willing to plan her death in retaliation. Each, as he plays out the reactions of sentiment in urgent and terrible projects, is at the same time held lightly in an irony of error: Ion thinks his mother to be unknown or the prophetess, his father to be Xuthus; Xuthus thinks Ion is his son and the mother unknown; the true mother is willing to credit any of these errors in her desperation.

Ion is so anxious about his parentage that he drops his initial clarity; Xuthus so wrapped up in his fatherhood that as the play unfolds he is distanced from the stage; Creusa so wrought up by past and present that she easily accedes to a murder crueler than Medea's.

But human folly is in touch with the gods at every point, first with the kind of accident—an unearthed cradle and swaddling bands—on which Hellenistic comedy later expanded for itself, but which here stands inextricably joined to other questions. Intention is muted, nobody really dies. Still, the sequence is presented as having great moment; Ion, whose name means the man who happens to "come" along the path, will be the forebear of all Athenians.

The omnipresent Apollo, absent from the play, has somehow diverted his temple servant and his oracle seekers into a familial relation that has nothing to do with the cult center to which it owes everything. The gods are present everywhere, sculpted in the friezes on the temple (184–216), woven into the tapestries Ion uses for his celebration (1141–56), and finally embroidered, by Creusa herself long ago, on the swaddling bands, at the center of which is the figure of the Gorgon, "edged with snakes like the aegis" (1421), whose blood has the double power of healing or killing (1003–6).

The prior mythological background is complex on Creusa's side, with the Erechtheus clan's involvement in death, sacrifice, and the war that brought her Xuthus, and the parallel story of the hidden son (271–75) that the daughters of Cecrops were not supposed to see. It is complex on Xuthus' side too, where the descent from Zeus through Aeolus brought him where he is. But these prior events do not operate dramatically in the play, as the prior events do in *Oedipus Rex* or the *Oresteia;* they merely suggest equivalent complexities wherever one turns. The gods complicate human life, or else people complicate it for themselves; city (Athens), cult (Apollo), and people (Ionians) are all tied up in these indeterminacies from their very origins. Creusa's statement to the young priest, who turns out later to be her son, accuses the god partially in a language that diverts itself to suggest justification:

τὰ κοινὰ χαίρων οὐ δίκαια δρᾷ μόνος.

Rejoicing in the common he does not do the just by himself.

(358)

This is meant in context to be a complaint, but rejoicing (χαίρων) is not in any easy antithesis either with doing (δρᾷ) or alone (μόνος), nor does "the common" (τὰ κοινὰ) balance or really contradict "the just" (δίκαια). Euripides' usual assertion of multiplicity for the demonic will not cover the cases here, though it does come up as a passing remark by the chorus, "many are the circumstances in many things for mortals / and the forms differ," (381–2). In the light of all these riddles, he closes with an assertion so simple that it has to be taken as ironic, a final testimony to the inexplicability of the events it has presented:

In the end the noble chance on worthy things,
And the bad, as they were born, do not fare well.

(1621–22)

The chorus here echoes Creusa, "Apart, the bad does not mix with the good" (1017). She is wrong, over the whole play. They are right, taking only the end. A fragment of the lost *Aeolus*[11] offers a counter-statement:

The noble and the bad should not be apart,
But there is a certain mixture, to have them right.

All is well at the end of the *Ion*, an advance has been made, the yearnings have been satisfied. The gods have not been vindicated. They are present everywhere; and yet they remain veiled, not in their presence, but in their ultimate operation.

5

"The form of events does not appear the same / When they are at a distance as when seen close at hand" (*Ion*, 585–86). Ion brings up this natural law of physical vision as an answer to Xuthus' offer of a kingship and wealth at Athens, applying it to things that are not physical. He is thus invoking, in dramatic irony, our application of the rule to his unwitting self; he will see differently by the end of the play.

In the *Ion* Apollo remains at a distance, but in the *Bacchae*, Dionysus has come from a distance and is close at hand. This gives quite a different cast to the form of events. Here, for the first and only time in Greek tragedy, the *deus ex machina*, later appearing in regular form (1330 ff.), comes early enough in the play to open it, to speak the prologue and be a main agent in the action.

In the presence of the stranger who turns out to be a god, the lives of the legendary rulers of Thebes are turned upside down, and with their own connivance. Euripides here returns to one episode prior to the panorama he had already presented in the *Phoenissai*. Dionysus has come, he tells us in the prologue, to redress the slight given him through his mother Semele, the daughter of Cadmus; the mother of king Pentheus, Agave, who is also the daughter of Cadmus, is induced to lead the frenzied group of bacchants onto a mountain, where she tears her son to pieces in the *sparagmos* of rending that animals have already undergone, something that Dionysus himself underwent in the "oldest" version of the myth. Pentheus has gone to the mountain at the seductive suggestion of Dionysus, who has freed himself from the king's prison by an earthquake, and he has put on women's clothing to disguise himself, taking on thereby an androgynous appearance ("woman-formed," θηλύμορφων, 353; also 451 ff.[12]) for which he has mocked the "smiling" (439) Dionysus. What Pentheus threatens against the figure he does not know to be his divine cousin, "to cut the neck apart from the body," (241) is inflicted on himself.

The orgy runs the gamut of an unnatural distortion of the mother-child relation that Dionysus had come to defend, from suckling the young of animals (699–700) to rending animals (734–45). This it does before it turns those symbolic ritual actions out of their path into the horrifying reality that kills Pentheus, crushes the waking Agave, and exiles her father for the long, further career prophesied by the god (1330–39).

The benign end, a "life in the land of the blessed" for Cadmus and Harmonia, contradicts, ambiguously (through another god—himself the god of war!), the destruction inherent in the manifested power of

Dionysus. It also reverses the initial movement from Asia to Europe (171–72). The bacchants had begun by considering only the benign side of the god; the benign release resulting from his ritual is a general one in the Greek world; the tragic festival celebrates it. And this enacted destruction is only a special case, the focus of a single legend— one which, however, must be given the generality that functions for any myth, and must be taken as the universal case for the spectators of this particular play.

The implicit contradiction between a benign rule and a malevolent single case is deployed into other dipolarities, to use the term which Charles Boer[13] applies to the play's presentation of polarities in its action. Boer stresses particularly the indeterminacy of the emotional overlay, the seemingly impossible fusion of grim tragic event and broad comedy throughout the action, from the entrance of the hoary Tiresias and Cadmus in bacchic garb (170–214), who are delighted to run off as old men to a festival usually reserved for young women, all the way to the terrifying appearance of Agave bearing on her thyrsus her son's head that she thinks to be a lion's. There has to be a comic effect in her summoning her dead son to come and behold the lion's head which is really his own (1212–15). But the "smile" on the actor's Dionysus mask here is also, and at the same time, a grimace, in Rosenmeyer's words.[14] Emotionally we have gone far beyond the *Ion's* tragicomic and faintly nostalgic yearning, from unawareness to awareness, of mother and son, an action this play powerfully telescopes in the desperate appeal of Pentheus to his deaf, frenzied mother. (1118–25). That yearning is redirected and inverted in the gentle, hopeless dialogue between that mother, now in the role of a daughter, and her old father Cadmus, as he brings her round to the awareness that will crush her (1231–1301). "Grief measureless and impossible to look at," (1244), Cadmus says, and that impossibility is invested emotionally in the heavy retranslation of horror into grim humor, without either Grand Guignol or tragic farce.

The measure of this measureless grief, in the spectator's emotions, is itself "measureless and impossible to look at." Agave clutching the false lion's head, caught in the irony of the audience, is ridiculously grotesque, but the horror freezes the ridicule, the ridicule deflects the horror. The Aphrodite and Artemis of the *Hippolytus*, the Athene and Poseidon of the *Trojan Women* have been conflated into one god who is not double-faced but single-faced behind the mask whose smile it is impossible to read.

The god is ambivalent in his relations to men, but the effects of those relations stand beyond ambivalence: the horrible is horrible, the ridiculous is ridiculous. When the same act is, as though impossibly, horrible and ridiculous at once, so that the spectators have been taken beyond even a fusion of pity and terror; then the answer is to be sought in the god, who gives no answer, and yet who unifies this action, serving the same central function of evocation that Oedipus does in *Oedipus Rex*. Dionysus refers everything back to Dionysus. It is destructive to face him partially, whether to welcome him in a self-deceptive longing for peace, as the chorus does ("to cease from care," 381), or to fight him for the "evils" of driving the women out of their homes, as Pentheus returns to Thebes to do (215 ff.). And yet by definition he cannot be faced wholly.

Only by the play can this be accomplished. It is hard for even a unified tragicomic effect to be more than episodic; the preparation for war of the old Iolaus in the *Children of Heracles* (796 ff.) is at once pitiable and funny in ways having little to do with the theme of that play. In the *Phoenissai*, with gratuitous complexity, Antigone is herself a bacchant (1754 ff.)! Here Dionysus, from beginning to end, refers everything back to himself; Euripides has left the multiplicity of divine representation, in which the god who gets the prologue is never the *deus ex machina*, and he has forced all his events on a single line, round a single divine cause, with the result that the events perplex even more, and even ambivalence offers no release of adequacy between emotion and event. "Many are the forms of demonic things," his chorus again chants in conclusion. Here there is only one *daimon*, Dionysus, who enters by declaring that he is instituting his rites "so that I may be a manifest *daimon* among mortals (ἵν' εἴην ἐμφανὴς δαίμων βροτοῖς, 22). Or so that he may "clearly be a *daimon*," as he clearly is—and at once. The tempo of the play itself carries the humor, and the terror, of the dis-proportionately quick and total effect this god brings about; he no sooner finishes his prologue than the chorus of maenads chants his praises in their entrance song.

And this *daimon* is the god of the dramatic festival, the patron of both comedy and tragedy. The play, as an act of worship, questions an act of worship by reviving, in a context offering both emotionally and intellectually an infinite problem, the ritual of which it transcends. Between the death of Pentheus, which we see, and the blessing of Cadmus, which we take on faith, there is no point of union other than the cause of both, Dionysus. Moreover, Cadmus is the grandfather not only of Pentheus, but of Dionysus himself. And this is a pre-Oedipal Thebes, of long, long ago, into which these new rites (216, 256, 272, 467) are being introduced. Pentheus is a fighter against god, a θεομαχής as the play calls him three times (45, 325, 1255). The last time it is his mother who says it, deploring the fact that he could not be "well-beasted" (εὔθηρος, 1253). In not being well-disposed towards the bestial ritual, he has become the "good beast" her words ironically designate, and she is holding it in her hands. Euripides locks these events so that he neither fights the god nor praises him; or rather, he does both, impossibly and successfully. As in the *Ion* (especially 840–62), and as in the quizzical thrust of the *Alcestis*, the alternative between life and death serves not as an ultimate but as the crucial determinant of some further ultimate racking of the life it radically questions, an ultimate for which the name *"theos"* pretends to cover, away from which the enacted events, like the name "daimon," unmask the pretense.

# Chapter Seven: DAIMON

What is called the "experience of death" has no reality at all as such, but must be interpreted as the positive and creative experience of sacrifice. Here is not a loss, experienced by the survivor and projected into the deceased, but rather an anticipated gain, constitutive for life itself, a meaning for the sake of which anything whatsoever must yield, including empirical existence as a whole. Man is not, as the philosopher Simmel has put it, "he who is one day to die," for man has this in common with plants and animals. Man is the creature which knows that it has its life for the sake of giving it to a higher fulfillment. Man's life is sacramental. In this way, man indeed lives perpetually in the presence of sacrifice and, if it must be, of death. Here is not a necessity, the "when" of which is accidental, but rather a necessarily free decision, experienced in the integration of the whole personality, its past, and its tendencies toward the future. The accidental "when" has vanished in the free decision, which is not a decision to live toward death, but to give everything one has in the present. What was in mythology a dim identity of necessity and chance, developed to absurdity, is here the freedom of decision.

In this way, impersonal, mythological fate is changed into individual, personal destiny.[1]

Die Sorgestruktur spricht nicht *gegen* ein mögliches Ganzsein, sondern ist die *Bedingung der Möglichkeit* solchen existenziellen Seinkönnens. Im Züge dieser Analysen wurde deutlich, dass im Phänomen der Sorge die existenzialen Phänomene von Tod, Gewissen und Schuld verankert liegen. *Die Gliederung der Ganzheit des Strukturganzen ist noch reicher und damit die existenziale Frage nach der Einheit dieser Ganzheit noch dringlicher geworden.*[2]

1

The *daimon* is a god acting in and upon man, the *theos* energized and, in the force of the encounter, nameless, except that it is a *daimon*. The epithet δαιμόνιε in Homer, coming in direct address as a vocative, expresses the wonder between one person and another. The person who calls someone else δαιμόνιε declares that the other can only be acting in a way that indicates the active presence of still another, a supernatural being. The term drops away as a vocative from tragedy, where the ground on which the enactment takes place is a holy precinct and the *daimon* is always in evidence through the masks. The progress of the tragic action, which Aristotle abstracts into a knotting and a loosing, *desis* and *lusis*, gains its varied force from the varied supercharging of human agents by the energy of divine beings in many forms; "many are the forms of δαιμόνια" as Euripides concludes again and again.

*Oedipus Rex* pushes this force to the second degree and turns it in on itself. Alone among extant plays does it consist of reactions to a complete prior cycle of human interaction with the divine: long ago the oracle of Apollo said that Oedipus would kill his father and marry his mother. The father and the mother reacted to the oracle by trying to avoid it, by trying to do away with him; but he has already killed his father and married his mother, as the audience knows from the myth at the outset. What is more, Oedipus has already reacted to the oracle in his own way; after consulting it on a trip to Delphi and hearing that he is to kill his father and marry his mother, he has abandoned Corinth forever. The play builds to the point of awareness, which is also the point of catastrophe (the *peripeteia* coinciding with the *anagnoris* in Aristotle's terms), the reactions to this ineluctable past.

Sophocles has performed the unique master stroke of taking the mysterious daimonic influence so for granted that he cannot only locate it prior to the action, as Knox points out,[3] but leave it utterly unexamined. The sacrifice of Iphigeneia in the *Agamemnon*, the judgment of Achilles' armor in the *Ajax*, the spurning of Semele in the *Bacchae*, the gift of Nessus in the *Trachiniai*—these prior acts are all given in a nexus of cause, and as cause they lead to further acts, to deaths. But the prior acts in the *Oedipus* lead only to an inquiry into their *existence*, not into their nature; not into what it means for Apollo to have prophesied this, or what effect he might have had in daimonically bringing about the murder and the incest. It is the inquiry into, and the reaction to, the prior acts that lead to the death of Jocasta and the self-blinding and exile of Oedipus. *Oedipus Rex* combines the situation of the *Ion* with the dreadful consequences of the *Bacchae*.

Another way of putting it would be to say that the nexus of cause is

total, the daimonic is all-embracing, and the enactment is so supercharged that the beings involved can only inquire—not just because the
action is past, but because its significance is total, beyond even the
major bind of Orestes, who, to revenge the murder of his father, must
murder his mother, and he does. The pastness of the action provides the
ground for the totality, and Sophocles' complete reliance on that
pastness provides the enactment of totality.

Freud's explanation is counter-Sophoclean in one sense; the explanation is exactly what Sophocles is unique for omitting, where even
the *Bacchae* provides an explanation of Dionysus in the form of a
dilemma about him. But unnamed Ares, who has silently sent the
plague upon Thebes, is never examined for why this particular
moment was chosen, and the silence that shrouds Apollo's complicity
in the events his oracle either foretold or foreordained stands unbroken
as the intial condition of the play. Freud breaks that silence with an
explanation of the prior events, but not of the events of the play.
Towards those, he is on the side of Jocasta:

> Already many mortals in their dreams
> Have shared their mother's bed. But he who counts
> This dream as nothing, easiest bears his life.     (981–83)

The healthy man, for Freud, is one who is easily bearing his life by
counting the Oedipus dream as nothing. Of course, in the play we have
not the case of everyman ("many mortals") who somehow dreams of
breaking the direst taboos, dire because they are magnets for those
dreams. Instead, we have the unique case of a man who has placed
himself beyond the taboos against parricide and incest by committing
them—in a way, however, that is the only way everyman would break
across from the dream into the reality, by not knowing what he was
doing.

Oedipus is everyman *par excellence*: he is a king, like the Pentheus
of the *Bacchae* or the Creon of the *Antigone*. He is faced not by some heavy
problematic incursion, of Dionysus or Aphrodite, but again, by himself,
by his own past. The everyman becomes the unique case, the myth is
daimonically supercharged into the aching fact, through the process of
enacted inquiry. Oedipus spans the distance from one role into another,
from head of the *polis* (ὑψίπολις, in the language of the *Antigone*) to out-

cast from the *polis* (ἄπολις), from a common to a unique fate, by asking
who has caused the plague, and by pursuing this inquiry relentlessly
against the advice of his motherly wife, in the face of the oracle Creon
brings, and in the teeth of the blind prophet whom not even the overweening Creon of the *Antigone* dares for a moment to withstand. He
surpasses Tiresias in prophetic power; he overturns the Sphinx that
had stopped the blind prophet (391–98). Now he is forced to enact
the mythic sense of that winged, deadly female by giving wings, so to
speak, to the past of the deadly female who shared his throne; he will
solve the riddle of the Sphinx and still encounter the disaster of those
who could not solve the riddle. He is himself, as De Quincey pointed
out,[4] the answer to the traditional riddle.

And now he must solve it not by special prophetic power, but by
steadfastly obeying a king's common duty towards his subjects. The
residuum of the special power is a common duty: the uniqueness that
brought him to the center obliges him to drive himself out into uniqueness again, and his impulse of anger against Tiresias evokes from the
chorus of Theban elders the ominous reaction of pity in the form of
inadequate definition:

> Terrible, terrible things the wise bird-augur stirs.
> I neither approve nor deny, at a loss for what to say . . .
> Zeus and Apollo surely understand and know
> The affairs of mortal men, but that a mortal seer
> Knows more than I, there is no proof. Though a man
> May surpass a man in knowledge,
> Never shall I agree, till I see the word, true, when men blame
> Oedipus,
> For there came upon him once clear the winged maiden
> And wise he was seen, by sure test sweet for the state.
> So never shall my mind judge him evil guilt.     (482–511)

His main thrust forward, in an impulsive anger momentarily outfaced
by the seemingly measured calm of the elders, will bring him well
beyond them, and beyond everyone else, to the fatal knowledge of who
and what he is. To solve the riddle he needs not knowledge but
ignorance; Jocasta and Tiresias would not act on that knowledge. The
effect of his ignorance is to lay his body, his substantive existence, on

the line, something his knowledge before the Sphinx had only risked in an uncertain future; where here, because of the past, disaster is not the possible consequence of not solving the riddle but the certain consequence of solving it.

Others on stage, at the very least Tiresias and the shepherd, already possess the crucial knowledge that Oedipus is the son of Jocasta, but it takes a complicated set of events to bring this information to light. And there is something of character-fatedness in the uniqueness of the man who carries out the inquiry. The action of searching it out is propelled by the will of Oedipus himself: his undoing is linked, in the dynamics of his action, to the very quality of resoluteness which had led him to the throne. The same decisiveness that caused him to flee from Corinth at the drunken taunt that he was not his father's son, to kill the threatening Laius, to solve the riddle of the Sphinx and marry Jocasta, also brings him to push on till he uncovers the truth of the fate underlying that decisiveness. At the end he moves, as he had done when he left Corinth—as well as when he went there—into a totally new sphere of life, but this time it is in full knowledge of the horrible circumstances that pollute him.

The play moves through the stages of the search, narrowing on the unambiguous revelation of Oedipus' contamination. As it does so, the play touches on many matters profoundly rooted in the assumptions of an early people: the slaying of a king by his successor, the testing of a hero by a supernatural beast, the connection between a king's sanctity and the physical health of his people, the validity of what a blind prophet says. The myth takes over, as its effects are being questioned.

At the beginning of the play, Oedipus stands close to the point where, in destroying the dramatic irony of the audience towards him, he will destroy the existence he has been straining to preserve. In the light of the audience's knowledge, that dramatic irony weights the speeches of the play moment by moment, and provides much of the instant power on the stage. The pastness of the main action, patricide and incest, functions to give the dramatic irony this special weight of reversal: the converging resolution of the irony does not open the character towards the release of knowledge, so that his enacted convergence with the audience group will be empowering—as it is for Ion, for the Theseus of the *Hippolytus*, for Hecuba, for Sophocles' Electra, and ultimately for the Heracles of the *Trachiniai*, for Philoctetes, and even for Admetus. Instead, when the irony is resolved, the man is broken—and this reversal of the usual function of irony accounts at least as fully as does the coincidence of *peripeteia* and *anagnorisis* for the tightness of the play; indeed, that Aristotelian coherence can itself be ascribed to this central dramaturgic strategy, whereby the normal circuit of identifications between actor, imagined scene, audience group, and actual life, is set going in a still more tragic way by intensifying it around this inversion of the usual process.

Without this irony the play would be simply pessimistic, and so in Lionel Abel's terms,[5] not tragic. We would simply "behold this Oedipus" in his "surge of dread fate," and would continue to stand off from him. But the motion of the drama has been to bring him round to the point where he fails precisely because he succeeds in finding out what we already know.

The irony dramatizes the act of identification between the actor and the audience, and at the same time thrusts him away, the other side of the taboo, beyond either the pity we could feel for the struggling king or the terror we could feel for the incestuous parricide. The point where he converges with the audience, to enact being everyman, is the point of his utter uniqueness. The closure of the myth's imagined scene is to open the real scene beyond pessimism by setting the common and the unique in Oedipus at odds precisely when the two are being equated through the convergence of the dramatic irony. He is in the whole of his life. Since he is Oedipus himself, he cannot be one who recognizes the enactment of the Oedipus myth. The asymptote of his circle—in the circular orchestra, we may fancifully say—is the center of our circle, and vice versa.

The tragedy locks. If the oracles mean nothing, "why must I dance the sacred dance?" (τί δεῖ με χορεύειν; 896) ask the Theban elders; and in the sacred dances, as part to whole, as real scene to imagined, as choral dance in the Athens of the Dionysiac festival under the form of ritual dance in Thebes, they touch on the inversion of the irony. "If the oracles and the truth do not coincide, the very performance of the tragedy has no meaning," Knox says.[6] "For tragedy is itself a form of worship of the gods. This phrase 'why should I dance?' is a *tour de force* which makes the validity of the performance itself turn on the

*dénouement* of the play." And the turn in this *tour de force* is intensified
because the reference inverts the usual relation of the imagined scene
to the real, for usually it is the real scene that is the whole, and the
imagined scene that is part thereof; whereas here the real ritual scene
must be reckoned as only part of the whole which would include all
forms of ritual dancing (what the Theban elders on stage must be
signifying by the verb χορεύειν, the whole class of dances including
dances done by choral actors—like themselves "really").

In the light of this overriding and strangely self-defeating dramatic
irony, the ideological contrasts in the play, which are ironic in another
sense, are drawn into the progress of an action that overmasters them.
Blindness and sight, power and helplessness, piety and irreverence,
health and sickness, enter the assertions of the characters and define
their positions in a way that is merely preliminary when the paradoxes
of linguistic assertion and stichomathic contention are subsumed under
the large paradox, this steady removal of dramatic irony. Into this
Oedipus lives his way out, into a terrible clarity where the act of
blinding himself because he sees is itself only preliminary to expulsion.
That itself is in turn preliminary to a purgative death he knows more
about than the audience, since that part of the myth is far more
obscure and *Oedipus at Colonus* will not be written for another quarter
of a century.

> And yet this much I know, neither a sickness
> Nor anything else can kill me. I would not
> Be saved from death, except for some dread evil.
> Well, let my fate go wherever it may.       (1455–58)

Of course he cannot violate the severe tone of this conclusion to see
his death in other than negative terms, an "awesome misfortune," as
the words could also be rendered.

Oedipus' intimation of his future, presented here only through a
vague qualification, nevertheless opens the end of the play beyond the
absoluteness of his expulsion by Creon and the totality of the cautionary
exemplum for which the chorus offers him. "Count no man happy till
he is dead," the chorus concludes, applying the principle specifically
to the events of this plot. But the principle subverts their application;
Oedipus has not yet seen his "final day"; in being the only character

who takes his future, however dimly, into account, he is also the only one who measures the full thrust of the action. He continues to be wise in his pitiable vacillation towards exile; they continue to need his mysterious leadership in ways that will not become clear till far in the future (as, again, the audience knows from the myth). The group of the final scene offers, then, not a final figure of the meaning of the enactment, but rather a powerful set that makes the sequence of this enactment suggest, finally, something equally powerful while utterly different. The opening of Oedipus's intimation in his statement above contains the seed of the same daimonic power, utterly transformed, which he had demonstrated both in taking over Thebes and in pursuing his inquiry at whatever cost.

The large dramatic irony, through its inversion of effect, dominates other possible ironies, and holds the enactment firmly at the center of whatever meaning the play propounds: it resists being returned to its paradoxes; it cannot be ideologized; and to explain its conditions with Freud, to see it for radical clinical insight, leaves the tragic sense of the play unplumbed. Or else is willing just to label "tragic" what it constructively enacts, not the unconscious, but the inevitable fault of consciously handling it.

A mortal man cannot be called blessed till he ends his life: this commonplace, far too widespread in Greece to be called simply Sophoclean, has been plumbed by the play, and it concludes with it, spelling out the unknown in time as the threat to bliss inherent in the fact of being mortal, a point of which the large irony has made an a fortiori demonstration:

> So I would say a mortal man, while he is watching
> To see the final day, can have no happiness
> Till he pass the bound of life, nor be relieved of pain.
> (1528–30)

And Oedipus has not yet passed the bound of life, he has only given a startling and all-embracing demonstration of what it may mean to be mortal.

Seen as in tension with the knowledge of the audience, Oedipus projects a steady resistance to the dramatic irony, and the play moves in an even line, its direction is straight. Seen as in pursuit of an unknown murderer, his unironic action on stage itself keeps raising its pitch; its direction is up, toward increasing tension. Each time, as he moves closer, he talks to someone more important for him, first to Creon, then to Tiresias, then to Jocasta. The maximal permitted complication of three actors is permuted, resolving to just the important two in the long second episode, the midpoint of the play.

Then, at this point of tightness, comes not the messenger sent for, the old Theban shepherd, but a surprising new arrival, the Corinthian messenger, whose coincidental earlier role in handing the infant Oedipus over to the king and queen of Corinth is soon capped by another crushing coincidence, that the man who escaped from the crossroads where Laius was murdered is the same man who got the infant Oedipus to hand over in the first place. This accidental fusion of roles into persons each of whom knows the other, and each of whom can produce, as it happens, not one but two pieces of information, may be taken to correspond to the main coincidence, as it seems: that the man whom Oedipus killed at the crossroads happened to be his father, happened to be king of the land he happened to go to, that Oedipus happened to marry the Queen who happened to be his mother—and we are back at the oracle, but at the same time all this startlingly and ironically illustrates Oedipus frenzied contention about a parentage no mortal can have, since everyone must have a real father and mother:

> I would not be dishonoured to call myself
> The Son of Fortune, giver of the good.
> She is my mother. The months, her other children,
> Have marked me sometimes small and sometimes great.
> Such was I born! I shall prove no other man,
> Nor shall I cease to search out my descent          (1080–85)

The last statement contradicts his assertion, as its extravagance verges on rivaling the gods. And he has ironically said this just after his real mother has said she has spoken her last words to him forever. Yet he is right; Fortune, *tuche*, has been present at every point of the coincidences, and about their fatality he is still in the dark.

The assertion stands in the ironic light of the fact that the joining coincidences are sundering ones: the two servants, coming together coincidentally, presenting their coincidentally doubled knowledge, prove that Oedipus equals Oedipus, the murderer is a parricide and also incestuous; and it is not till he has discovered the true definition of the crime he already knows he has committed, that he discovers the existence of the other crime towards a woman who has ironically seen it herself and rushed off to kill herself to avoid facing facts she is quite content simply to know.

Mortal man suffers his identity. Oedipus, finding it in losing it, is seen as projecting the suffering into a time progression that has negated time:

> Who so lives in wild plagues, who dwells in pains,
> In utter change of life?
> Alas for glorious Oedipus!
> The selfsame port of rest
> Was gained by bridegroom father and his son,
> How, O how did your father's furrows ever bear you,
>     suffering man?
> How have they endured silence for so long?
>
> You are found out, unwilling, by all-seeing Time.
> It judges your unmarried marriage where for long
> Begetter and begot have been the same.          (1205–15)

This lamentation of the chorus comes just after all has been revealed, and just before the suicide of Jocasta and the self-blinding of Oedipus are to be announced by the entering messenger. The even progression of time hides an event which negates man's subjection to time. As a person, and in the traditional riddle of the Sphinx, as the one who walks differently at the morning, the noon, and the evening of the day which is his life, a man's mortal existence inexorably moves ahead, like the play, into the future when he will die. At the same time, though, he exists in a cyclical series of generation: he is at once a son and a father, he belongs to a family, and that membership stamps his mortality as more than the linear series that Oedipus has invoked when he says of *tuche* that "the months, her other children, / Have marked me sometimes small and sometimes great."

"Alas, generations of mortal men!" the chorus has begun in the stasimon cited above, "How equal to nothing do I number you in life!" By his double ignorant crime, that the tightness of the drama exemplifies as well as presents, in the inexorable progression of time, Oedipus has also negated time. He has mixed up the generations; he has provided the occasions for saying that they are equal to nothing. In suffering the uniqueness of his identity he has been unique in confounding it.

The play returns again and again to questions of time, and the conclusion emphasizes repeatedly the horrible surplus of identity invoked when "begetter and begot have been the same": in the messenger's speech (1245–50); in Oedipus' own description (1359–61); and again in his longer statement (1402–6); and still again in the subversion of human terminology when he speaks to his daughters:

> My children, where are you? Come to me, come
> Into your brother's hands, that brought about
> Your father's eyes, once bright, to see like this.   (1480–83)

Creon himself, for all his complexity of managing to keep to one side of the catastrophe at every turn, does refer, in the newly assured tact of his beginning rule, to the same principle, but delicately:

> If you defer no longer to mortal offspring,
> Respect at least the all-nourishing flame
> Of Apollo, lord of the sun.   (1424–26)

When Oedipus has shown Apollo the respect (*aidos* is the substantive term), first of prayer (80–81) and finally of horrified recognition, to the Chorus's question "What *daimon* drove you on?" he has replied, "Apollo it was, Apollo, friends." (1329–30). The notion that Oedipus may "defer no longer to mortal offspring" (καταισχύνεσθε; "be ashamed before") brings Creon's language to the ground on the other side of taboo by which Oedipus is at once accursed and sacred.

Seen schematically, with reference to the timelessness of the myth, people on that ground strain, in Girard's formulation,[7] to avoid the deadly symmetry of identification involved in the necessary reciprocity of violence—except towards the scapegoat, Oedipus in this case. In his case the point of symmetry is first touched and then—in the touching and by the fact—denied ritually, so as to avoid the total suffering of identity. In this formulation, Creon and Oedipus are "enemy brothers," and the son is the brother of his own father, as Oedipus's incest has made him. Girard sees the limping of Oedipus as an acknowledgement in the myth of the impossibility of absolutizing this symmetry: Oedipus, everyman, stumbles before the stumbling block, the *skandalon* (to use the Greek term which occurs in noun and verb forms forty-four times in the New Testament, once with a different sense in Aristophanes, but never once in all Greek tragedy) of the interchanging trouble between symmetry and dissymmetry. "The expulsion has for its object to assure its own misunderstanding," he says. And further, "The difference produced by the *skandalon* creates avoidances and gaps which anticipate rivalry or neutralize it: this difference takes the concrete form of taboos, hierarchic distinctions, and institutions which prevent the convergence of desires and destroy the possibilities of confrontation."[8]

Still, it is only in the schematism of the myth, seen atemporally, or it is only by emphasizing in the presentness of episodes, as Girard does, Oedipus's confrontations with Creon and Tiresias (but not Jocasta), that Oedipus's universality can be separated from his uniqueness, his "symmetry" with all men from his utter dissymmetry. In the doubling irony of the play's relentless time, he encompasses these possibilities in his person; he is that and more. He is not merely a scapegoat who stands on the other side of the taboo: the daimonic dynamism of the events of self-realization that put him there constitute themselves a realization, not an avoidance, for anyone. We face the play squarely; if we do not, its meaning cannot be that we do not see it.

Systematic thought, being atemporal, must lay itself open to the hidden *skandalon* of its premises. Freud, in Girard's view, has the son "erect . . . the superego . . . to escape the *skandalon*"[9] and he "cannot conceive of rivalry without the hostility of the son; he cannot dissociate rivalry and *consciousness* of rivalry." But in this play these opposites are reconciled by the bending of self-search on a single ironic time-line. Oedipus does perform this dissociation nearly all the way: he is always confronting Creon, always confronting the consequences of what Tiresias has said, and at the same time he is always coming back to a past whose pastness takes its meaning, not from dissymmetry between himself and his father, but from a symmetry which can have its meaning only if the sequence which itself is a mortally absolute dissociation of familial past from egoistic present has not been confounded—and it has. His brotherhood with his father is a subverting horror, not a liberating realization, though the horror, indeed, is mastered and envisioned by the controlling enactment of the play.

In his handling of the taboo with which the play is interwoven at many points, the figure of Oedipus involves beliefs at once "primitive and Olympian," in the words of Thalia Feldman.[10] There, at the end of the play, on the other side of further identities, isolated at the terrible end of a clarified life, his death is in view. Mortality and the gods have left this stage terribly clear. At the beginning, the oracle of Apollo, a revelation given a generation before, is present in its horror. Everyone may understand how powerfully the *daimon* may condemn incest and parricide. No one understands fully what may happen the other side of that condemnation, except by winning through the search that constitutes the play. The end defines all the action preceding, and all that precedes the action. "Pride breeds the tyrant," the chorus evasively says just after it seems clear that Oedipus himself is at least the murderer he has been seeking. But before this the chorus seems to be caught up—these are Theban elders not unlike the Athenian ones who may be watching the play—in a civic wisdom that bears the marks of the events' visionary spell, as Creon's tone and utterances do at the end. In the same metrical form and colametric position as "Pride breeds the tyrant" (a limited, past-set formula), they invoke the mortal identity of fate while upholding the pureness (ἁγνεία) which Oedipus himself never abandons in all the horror— though this exact word does not come up another time in the play, or in all of Sophocles:

εἴ μοι ξυνείη φέροντι
μοῖρα τὰν εὔσεπτον ἁγνείαν λόγων
ἔργων τε πάντων, ὧν νόμοι πρόκεινται
ὑψίποδες, οὐρανίαν
δι' αἰθέρα τεκνωθέντες, ὧν Ὄλυμπος
πατὴρ μόνος, οὐδέ νιν
θνατὰ φύσις ἀνέρων
ἔτικτεν, οὐδὲ μήποτε λάθα κατακοιμάσῃ·
μέγας ἐν τούτοις θεός οὐδὲ γηράσκει.

May fate come on me as I bear
Holy pureness in all word and deed,
For which the lofty-striding laws were set down,
Born through the heavenly air
Whereof the Olympian sky alone the father was;
No mortal spawn of mankind gave them birth,
Nor may oblivion ever lull them down.
Mighty in them the god is, and he does not age;     (863–71)

Man has another father than the Olympian sky alone, and he is not born through the heavenly air but of a mortal spawn; he ages. Yet he can envision, as well as obey, the lofty-striding laws in which the god is mighty. This god here is a *theos*, not a *daimon*, but the effects of the *daimon* have to be seen before the loftiness of those laws can be realized. Out of reach in their habitation among the immortals, they remain in view.

## 2

Mortal man cannot know his own death directly; he only knows that he is mortal. Since optimism or pessimism must be based on a reading of what one knows, death as a central and final event transcends both optimism and pessimism. The "tragic sense of life" derives not only positively from man's universal mortality, but negatively, in so far as it is a sense that transcends a reading of the known; in both ways it goes beyond the optimism or pessimism that, as Lionel Abel points out, must attend a reading of the known.

The sacrificial figure who takes his mortality upon himself, whether consciously or not, is then ejected into an unknown; the taboo is untouchable by the mind and heart. Its sacredness—*sacer* means untouchable—is tied up in its unapproachableness, just as the universality of death is tied up in its unknowability.

Death in tragedy is approached by plumbing the conditions under which a death may come to a man in a special way. In Renaissance tragedy, English or French, the special way derives from the values of the character; the depth at which the values of Hamlet or Othello, Brittanicus or Phèdre, are plumbed, itself has the darkness of a taboo area. We almost can say we feel someone is to die because the area of enacted discourse charges itself as some "dead vast and middle of the night," a strange and holy sequence. This may or may not involve the Hegelian principle of the good colliding with the good, as it does in *Coriolanus*, where the value of integrity and the value of patriotism tragically collide.

In Greek tragedy, to oversimplify, it is the *daimon* that causes the protagonist to miss the mark (the simple sense of Aristotle's *hamartia*); there is no plumbing of conditions and values, only a presentation, whose parity becomes the plumbing of them.

The conditions themselves, enacted in the sunlight before a ritual audience, carry their own overtones of the unknown. For men whose central unknown is their mortality, the enactment produces the tragic sense of life.

In *Oedipus at Colonus*, the protagonist stands close to death, and he has also been living for long years as someone who has gradually accustomed himself to the taboo. The approach of his death, as the city has wearied of him and sent him into exile, suddenly activates the antinomic force of the taboo by casting its holy side in the light of the benefit that Oedipus's death can bring for the city where he dies. He had heard this as a part of the old oracle from Apollo that had not entered the dramatic chain until his death is near: he will "furnish gains to those who receive me" (92). And there is also a new oracle, received by the Thebans, which puts this same information in negative form, "your tomb will be heavy for those among whom it fares ill" (402). The Thebans, under the management of Creon, wish to handle administratively the negative aspect of the taboo, as well as the positive; to put him in a fixed position close enough to help, and yet outside their borders:

> To stand you near the Cadmeian land, so that
> They may rule you, but you not enter the city's bounds
> (399–400)

Still, the oracle has also stated that he is to die in Athens' grove of the Furies—goddesses who have themselves a negative side that is insisted on (δεινῶπες, "dread-eyed," 84) as well as the positive side, the benign Eumenides who are "holy" (σεμνῶν, 90).

In the oracles, in the taboo, in the Furies, and therefore in the gods
of ambivalent myth, the negative cannot be extricated from the positive
by any management, the optimism from the pessimism. The tragic
wholeness of the enactment derives a serenity from the unparadoxical
handling of these fusions; in Oedipus's person, fatigue is inseparable
from mastery, and serenity imbues the very place where he arrives:

> This place is sacred, it would seem, and bursting
> With laurel, olive and the vine. Still thicker
> Within it are the fine-voiced nightingales          (16–18)

Here Antigone's praise is connected with the sacredness later emphasized by the Athenian stranger ("this whole place is sacred," 54), after
he has made it clear that it is the "fearful goddesses, maidens of Earth
and Darkness" (39–40) who possess it. This serenity is embodied in the
green glades, nightingale, narcissus, golden-gleaming crocus, bright
olive trees, and flowing streams of a real Athens. It is associated by the
chorus, as they welcome Oedipus there in their first *stasimon* (668–719)
with Dionysus (679) Aphrodite (693), Zeus (705), Athene (706) and
Poseidon (713), as well as with Demeter and Persephone (683–4). The
description is given in the form of an invitation to the Oedipus who
suggests that Apollo (665) may have sent Theseus to him. The plethora
of gods, invested in the city, have put that action of a daimon into the
far past as a central fact manageable in all its direness because the
direness, too, will become benign.

It is a stranger to the Thebans, the legendary ruler of the home city
of the dramatic audience, who brings all this about: Oedipus, in the
long past, could be Theban *par excellence*, the king, only by being a
non-Theban; and when he is discovered to be not a stranger, but
a Theban, after all, he has to become a stranger in the deeper sense
of a Theban who is taboo. These terms have now been transposed:
the alien city receives him with a charged version of that piety which
the home city should accord old men, as those who are about to
die. Being taboo makes Oedipus's mortality problematic, as it purges
his family relations into either civic ones (less than familial) or personal
ones (something more), either hostility from his sons and uncle or
devotion from his daughters. The family set is polarized into positive

or negative; the family only works if it honors him without using him. The desire to use him subverts itself, and the political purpose of good management, which generally asserts its value—in Oedipus's search for the murderer, or in Philoctetes' final aid to the Greeks—is here confounded by the mysteries that quietly transcend it.

The Athenians, represented by the chorus and by Theseus himself, do not master these mysteries; they only accept them in their midst. The result of this play's action will not provide the sort of concrete institution that the courts of the Areopagus become under the Eumenides at the end of the *Oresteia*. The result remains an unknown, a benign force associated with the gods. The tremendous trilogic resolution has been evened out into the calm of waiting acceptance that Oedipus enacts. The event can only be handled by being matched. He has ceased to suffer his identity, and the Athenians can gain from him by accepting that cessation; to challenge it is to incur the defeat of his challenger Creon or the curse that falls on his sons.

Oedipus's reply, when he hears from Ismene of his "powers" (κράτη, 392), is to assert that his identity as a man has come about through its non-existence; he has become himself through the taboo:

When I no longer am, just then I am a man?     (393)

To which her answer is true as well as truistic:

The gods have righted you, who ruined you before. (394)

And though he protests somewhat, he has said in his opening soliloquy that sufferings have taught him to στέργειν, a word which means "to love" and also "to be content or patient, to acquiesce." And not only his suffering, but just the mere passage of the time here shown easing into its long end; and as well as sufferings and time, "the noble quality.":

στέργειν γὰρ αἱ πάθαι με χὠ χρόνος ξυνὼν
μακρὸς διδάσκει, καὶ τὸ γενναῖον τρίτον.

Sufferings teach me to love, and the long
Time together, and, a third thing, nobility.     (7–9)

These qualities, triangulated heroically in the ultimate acceptance of an old man who has lived beyond the consequences of meeting ignorance for Sphinx-upsetting knowledge and taboo for kingship, are set at the beginning of the play as an ineluctable, unqualified fact, of which the ruptures in acceptance, and the occasional defections in the protagonist, will be slowly enacted to the foreknown benign point of the oracle.

The vision is that of the audience, since Oedipus, the only person who has it on stage, is blind, a fact he associates with his age when he speaks of himself as "a blind old man" in the first line of the play. There is not irony here, and little foreknowledge in the audience to produce it. Rather the blindness, whose disempowering quality he emphasizes (496) as an "evil," is the external signature not of the distant act that produced it; though that taboo comes to a head in the self-inflicted incapacity. Instead, the blindness, a masking of the mask so to speak, takes over the normal dramatic irony and renders it null in the overriding serenity.

Between blindness and sight in the actual scene of life, there is an essential difference, as there is between the ignorance of a character on stage and the knowledge of the audience. But between the blindness on stage and the vision, physical and spiritual, of the gripped audience for this play, the difference is inessential. As the play opens, it has been purged by Oedipus's life into an old age that has nullified the taboo as a preparation for godlike benignity. The purging of one difference (blindness–sight) justifies, in the progressively enacted emotions, the removal of another (dramatic irony).

Oedipus has achieved an acceptance that finds its full rhythmic form in the chorus's welcome to a fruitful, peaceful, and god-protected Athens (668–719) before Creon approaches to use other terms and call the city "powerful" and "great" (734). His diplomatic attempts, pitched in the dialectic of his speech, get none of the dramatic leverage here that the opponents of the suppliants manage in the *Suppliants* of Aeschylus or the *Children of Heracles* of Euripides. His "subtle machination of a just reason" (λόγου δικαίου μηχάνημα ποικίλον, 762) is at once named and rejected by Oedipus.

The sternness of the play's conclusion, by coming after the realized peace of acceptance (instead of before it in a normal order), is subordinated to the constancy of serene steadfastness in the taboo-releasing protagonist. The dramatic sequence presents a force assailing a peace, a civic and human power pitted against a psychic and god-ridden approach to death. Oedipus's own conviction brings him to reverse the power of Creon, and Creon's final expulsion of him before the play, by asking the good Athenians to "drive the impious man from this land" (ἐξελᾶτε τὸν ἀσεβῆ τῆσδε χθονός, 823). This expulsion does come about, after a struggle for power between Thebans and Athenians.

That the host city wins, and not the old man's home city, transposes the debate and the physical struggle (720–1043) into the realm of a subjection to something more than civic. But the winning city remains the Athens of the play's enactment. The praise of Athens and Theseus' magniloquent embodiments of civic virtue play into an end that comes as a *deus ex machina* comes, unexpectedly and through divine agency.

Still the disappearance, death, and apotheosis of Oedipus, the last event of the play, occurs in an *absence*. There is no god to explain, no *daimon* to whom the action may be ascribed. The Furies / Eumenides hold at the center of their grove a mysterious absence that pulls all virtues and pieties, all the antinomies of taboo and curse, all expiated guilt, away into an imagined scene that, through this enactment, carries a tragic sense to the heart of the real scene, the life into which the audience reenters after having experienced the enactment of *Oedipus at Colonus*, where the real Colonus has a real grove.

Oedipus's earlier preparation for death has been to yield to the simple pious request of Antigone, that he receive the praying stranger who turns out to be the Polyneices he will curse. He gets bitterly beyond the dramatic irony about Antigone's dedication to her brother, which the audience knows of from the myth. Antigone's appeal itself is made to an Oedipus whose deep serenity she has shared by fostering it, by sacrificing her own Theban life to serving as his eyes. The emotion of her request contains in itself the transcendence of Polyneices' fury: "Therefore the daimon looks at you" (τοιγάρ σ᾽ ὁ δαίμων εἰσορᾷ, 1370), Oedipus says to Polyneices, "And not yet the way it will" (1371) when the brothers lock in mortal combat, lost in their warring purposes beyond the power of Antigone or the will of Oedipus to save them.

She herself gets from her father, as the audience does, the resolution of mortality beyond the power of the daimonic to do other than happen. The piety of an existence goes deeper than the piety of a prayer, the enacted existence of the play surpasses, in a religious dynamic as well as a literary one, the act of worship the play begins to question and finally ceases to question.[11] The tragic sense has persisted through it.

The Athenians on stage, converging with the Athenians in the audience (and ourselves), are to be well-*daimoned*, or "blest" in remembering him:

> εὐδαίμονες γένοισθε, κἀπ' εὐπραξίᾳ
> μέμνησθέ μου θανόντος εὐτυχεῖς ἀεί.

> Be blest, and when you are faring well,
> Remember me, ever-fortunate, when I die.   (1554–55)

Of him they in turn say that a just *daimon* may increase him in recompense for the "vain sorrows" he suffered in the past and his daughters suffer at the coming news of his death:

> πολλῶν γὰρ ἂν καὶ μάταν
> πημάτων ἱκνουμένων
> πάλιν σφε δαίμων δίκαιος αὔξοι.

> For the many and vain
> Sufferings come upon him,
> May a just daimon in return prosper you   (1565–67)

This wish, spoken after his eternal disappearance from the stage, must refer to his unknown future, and, in shared feeling, to theirs. The sharing is civic and more than civic: Oedipus vanishes while actually holding the hand of Theseus, the ideal ruler. "All these things," they end by saying, "have κῦρος" (1778), a "validity" that implies an absolute "mastery," a dominion more than the one that his own coping skillful control as ruler of Thebes could have managed. The tragic sense distills out of itself a valid mastery that provides its own pacification, where a beginning of tensions already reconciled leads to an end of a blessing whose simplicities have been purged by the surprisingly full residues of a seemingly exhausted myth.

# NOTES

## INTRODUCTION

1. Thucydides, 2. 19–56.
2. Ibid., 2. 56. 5.
3. Knox, *Oedipus at Thebes*, Chapter II, "Athens," pp. 53–106. Knox shows how elaborately Oedipus as a person in *Oedipus Rex* recapitulates the traits of the city where the performance took place; consistently, then, all the individual bearing of the play can be extrapolated into the political realm. Oedipus' devotion to the *polis* of Thebes is implicitly only a part of what can wholly be applied to the *polis* of Athens.
4. John H. Finley, *Thucydides*, Cambridge, Mass., 1942, pp. 51, 55, 134.
5. Philip Whaley Harsh, *A Handbook of Classical Drama*, Stanford, 1965 [1944], pp. 45–46. [Stanford paperback].
6. William Arrowsmith, "Euripides' Theatre of Ideas," *Euripides*, ed. Erich Segal, Englewood Cliffs, N.J., 1968, pp. 27–31. [Spectrum paperback].
7. Thucydides, 2. 9. 3.
8. G. Zuntz, *The Political Plays of Euripides*, Manchester, 1963 [1955], pp. 97–104.
9. Thucydides, 2.9.2.
10. J. P. Vernant, *Les Origines de la pensée grecque*, Paris, 1962, p. 48.
11. J. L. Austin, *How to Do Things with Words*. The "William James Lectures" delivered at Harvard University, 1955. New York, 1965.
12. Ibid., p. 147.
13. Thomas Rosenmeyer, "Ajax: Tragedy and Time," *The Masks of Tragedy*, Austin, 1963, pp. 153–98.
14. G. W. F. Hegel, *Aesthetik*, Frankfurt, n.d. 1957 [1842], II, 564 ff. and passim.
15. A. W. Verrall. *Euripides: The Rationalist*, Cambridge, 1913.
16. Sigmund Freud, *Die Traumdeutung*, Vienna, 1950 [1900], p. 180.
17. Sir Richard Jebb, *Sophocles: The Plays and Fragments*, VII (Ajax), xxxvii ff.
18. Ignacio Errandonea, S. J., *Sofocles: Investigaciones sobre la estructura dramatica de sus siete tragedias y sobre la personalidad de sus coros*, Madrid, 1968, pp. 299–350.
19. Fridericus Ellendt, *Lexicon Sophocleum*, Berlin, 1872, sub voc.
20. Aristotle, *Poetics*, 1455b, 6–7.
21. Aristotle, *Poetics*, 1452a, 5–6.
22. Aristotle, *Poetics*, 1449a, 15–21.
23. Gerald Else, *Aristotle's Poetics*, Cambridge, Mass., 1963.
24. H. F. Cherniss, *Aristotle's Criticism of Presocratic Philosophy*, Baltimore, 1935.
25. Freud, *Die Traumdeutung*, 179–83.

26. Whether in actor or spectator, the *final* theoretical force is the same.
27. Claude Lévi-Strauss, *Les Structures élémentaires de la parenté*, Paris, 1949.
28. Theodor H. Gaster, *Thespis: Ritual, Myth, and Drama in the Ancient Near East*, New York, 1961.
29. Gilbert Murray, "Excursus on the Ritual Forms Preserved in Greek Tragedy," in *Themis: A Study of the Social Origins of Greek Religion* by Jane Ellen Harrison, London, 1963 [1912], p. 353. He spells it out as follows, 343–44: "If we examine the kind of myth which seems to underlie the various 'Eniautos' celebrations [and the structure of Greek plays] we shall find:
    1. An *Agon* or Contest, the Year against its enemy, Light against Darkness, Summer against Winter.
    2. A *Pathos* of the Year-Daimon, generally a ritual or sacrificial death, in which Adonis or Attis is slain by the tabu animal, the Pharmakos stoned, Osiris, Dionysus, Pentheus, Orpheus, Hippolytus torn to pieces (σπαραγμός).
    3. A *Messenger*. For this Pathos seems seldom or never to be actually performed under the eyes of the audience. (The reason of this is not hard to suggest, and was actually necessary in the time when there was only one actor.) It is announced by a messenger. 'The news comes' that Pan the Great, Thammuz, Adonis, Osiris is dead, and the dead body is often brought in on a bier. This leads to
    4. A *Threnos* or Lamentation. Specially characteristic, however, is a clash of contrary emotions, the death of the old being also the triumph of the new . . .
    5 and 6. An *Anagnorisis*—discovery of recognition—of the slain and mutilated Daimon, followed by his Resurrection or Apotheosis or, in some sense, his Epiphany in glory. This I shall call by the general name *Theophany*. It naturally goes with a *Peripeteia* or extreme change of feeling from grief to joy.
    Observe the sequence in which these should normally occur: *Agon, Pathos, Messenger, Threnos, Theophany*, or we might say, *Anagnorisis* and *Theophany*."

## CHAPTER 1: MYTHOS

1. Ernst Cassirer, *Philosophie der symbolischen Formen*, II, Darmstadt, 1964, p. 291 and passim.
2. James Hillman, *Emotion*, London, 1962.
3. Edward T. Hall. *The Silent Language*, Greenwich, Conn., 1961 [1959; Fawcett paperback]. Robert Ardrey, *Territorial Imperative*, New York, 1966.
4. This point was made by Irving Feldman in an oral comment at a Colloquium, Buffalo, 17 February 1969.
5. T. W. Adorno, *Jargon der Eigentlichkeit: Zur Deutschen Ideologie*, Frankfurt, 1964, p. 29. "Vollendete Entmythologisierung bringt Transzendenz ganz auf die Abstraktion, den Begriff."
6. Cassirer, op. cit., p. 82. "Daher sind die Relationen, die er setzt, keine gedanklichen Bindungen, durch welche das, was in sie eingeht, zugleich gesondert und verknüpft wird, sondern sie sind eine Art von Kitt, der auch das Ungleichartigste noch irgendwie zusammenzuleimen vermag."

7. Claude Lévi-Strauss, *Le Cru et le cuit*, Paris, 1964, p.20.
8. Claude Lévi-Strauss, *Anthropologie structurale*, Paris, 1958, pp. 235–42.
9. Claude Lévi-Strauss, *Du Miel au cendres*, Paris, 1966, p. 408.
10. Bruno Snell, *The Discovery of the Mind*, New York, 1960, p. 94. [Harper Torchbook ed.].
11. H. D. F. Kitto, *Greek Tragedy*, Garden City, N.Y., 1952, pp. vi-vii [1954; Anchor Books ed.]. "The 'meaning' contained in many a dramatic speech or chorus may be as direct as the 'meaning' of a passage in Aristotle's *Ethics*, but that 'meaning' which alone will explain the form of the play is something more akin to the 'meaning' of a Rembrandt or of a Beethoven sonata."

    Snell, op. cit., p. 98. Modern aesthetic presuppositions confuse Snell, in the passages I italicize here:

    "The standard of truth and falsehood which was appropriate to the epic is wholly out of place here. A new perspective of reality appears to be in the making.

    "During the early days of tragedy this change in the relation between artefact and reality is noticeable also in the products of Athenian art. B. Schweitzer has drawn our attention to the fact that in the statuary inscriptions of the early period the image is quite simply identified with the person portrayed: that statue is the man. Thus we may read on a figure: 'I am Chares, the ruler of Teichiousa.' In Attica, however, the usual phrasing is: 'I am the image, the grave stele, or the memorial stone of such and such a man.' Here we have proof that in Athens the work of art is no longer naively declared to be one with the model. *That means that the visual arts are conceived as a sphere apart*; art, instead of being identical with reality, dissociates itself from its domain. It imitates reality, represents it, signifies it—and thereby becomes a different sort of reality itself. *The process is the same in the realm of tragedy*; it is not until art has broken with reality that we get an expansion of the circle of subjects, a freer variation of themes. Not until this moment was art able to unfold itself without impediment. On the other hand—and again the parallel with tragedy is obvious—sculpture needed to travel a long way before it reached its objective of totally unhampered invention. For, to repeat ourselves, serious art may no longer be interested in portraying reality, but neither does it lie. Although the myths of tragedy gradually turn into a jungle of new plots, the 'play at first retains as much as possible of the ancient 'reality'; it retains a certain proximity to fact, and therein it differs from the sailors' yarns and from comedy."

    Snell sees something of moment here, but he distorts it when he aestheticizes it. The function of the statue remained "unaesthetic": it existed intentionally as a grave marker. And, similarly, a Greek play exists intentionally as an act of Panhellenic devotion to Dionysus. The statue inscription and the Greek play alike compel our admiration just because they transformed the structure of their signification while retaining their social matrix of intentionality. That the new structure does *not* give a new matrix preserves the essential character of the object within the society.
12. The ensuing psychological complications in the spectator are well described by André Green, *Un Oeil en trop*, Paris, 1969, pp. 13–14:

"Mais, comme le but du spectacle n'est certainement pas d'enfermer ses participants dans une solitude solipsiste, ni non plus d'en restreindre les effets par une extériorité mutuelle de ses parties, il faut en rendre compte par une autre opération. Ce renvoi à la source à mis néanmoins celle-ci en rapport avec l'objet du spectacle que le regard a rencontré en outrepassant la barrière de la rampe . . . . Ce retournement sur soi va s'accompagner d'un deuxième renversement—retournement en son contraire—qui est d'une signification plus difficile à saisir. Le premier renversement a, pour ainsi dire, donné la mesure de l'altérité fondamentale du spectacle à l'égard du spectateur. Si le spectateur consentait à cette altérité, il s'en irait ou s'endormirait et ce serait la fin d'un spectacle qui n'aurait jamais commencé."

13. Sigmund Freud, "Die Masse und die Urhorde," in *Das Unbewusste: Schriften zur Psychoanalyse*, ed. S. Fischer, Berlin and London, 1950, p. 278.
14. Lévi-Strauss, *Le Cru et le cuit*, p. 36.
15. Norman O. Brown, *Life Against Death*, New York, 1959 [1961; Vintage Books].
16. Herbert Weisinger, *Tragedy and the Paradox of the Fortunate Fall*, East Lansing, Mich., 1953, p. 29.
17. Mario Praz, *The Romantic Agony*, London, 1960 [1933].
18. Frederich Nietzsche, *Die Gebürt der Tragödie, Nietzsches Werke*, Saltzburg, n.d., I, 607.
19. Erich Neumann, *The Origins and History of Consciousness*, I, New York, 1954, [1962; Harper Torchbook ed.].
20. Geza Roheim, *The Riddle of the Sphinx; or, Human Origins*, London, 1934.
21. Georges Dumézil, *Mythe et épopée*, Paris, 1968, and *Jupiter Mars Quirinus*, Paris, 1941.
22. Lévi-Strauss, *Le Cru et le cuit*, p. 155. "Alors, l'analyse structurale reposerait entièrement sur des pétitions de principe, et elle perdrait sa seule justification, qui réside dans le codage à la fois unique et le plus économique, auquel elle sait réduire des messages dont la complexité était fort rebutante et qui, avant qu'elle n'intervienne, semblaient impossibles à déchiffrer.
23. Mircea Eliade, *Aspects du mythe*, Paris, 1963.
24. Norman O. Brown, *Love's Body*, New York, 1966 [Vintage Books].
25. Ibid., p. 219. "Figures are always figures of last things; typology (symbolism) is eschatology."
26. Northrop Frye, *Anatomy of Criticism*, Princeton, 1957, p. 192. Or to put it in the formal terms of another literary vocabulary with Geoffrey Hartman, *Yale French Studies*, 36–37, October, 1966, p. 159, n. "His archetypes are underdetermined as principles of structure and overdetermined as poetic symbols."
27. John P. Brown, "Literary Contexts of the Common Hebrew-Greek Vocabulary," *Journal of Semitic Studies*, 13 (Autumn 1968), 184–87, connecting the Greek griffin with the winged cherub guarding the Ark of the Covenant.
28. A. W. Pickard-Cambridge, *Dithyramb Tragedy and Comedy*, rev. by T. B. L. Webster, Oxford, 1966 [1962], p. 124. Zenob. v. 40. "Nothing to do with Dionysus. When, the choruses being accustomed from the beginning to sing the dithyramb to Dionysus, later the poets

abandoned this custom and began to write Ajaxes and Centaurs. Therefore the spectators said in joke, 'Nothing to do with Dionysus.' For this reason they decided later to introduce satry-plays as a prelude, in order that they might not seem to be forgetting the god."

29. See also Heraclitus' startling assertion "Hades and Dionysus are the same," (ὡυτὸς δὲ Ἀΐδης καὶ Διόνυσος), *Die Fragmente der Vorsokratiker*, Diels-Kranz, Berlin, 1960 [1952], I, 155.

30. Walter F. Otto, *Dionysus: Myth and Cult*, Bloomington, 1965. See also Lewis Richard Farnell, *The Cults of the Greek States*, V, Oxford, 1907, especially pp. 113–14, A. B. Cook, *Zeus: A Study in Ancient Religion*, Cambridge, 1914, 1925, and Martin Nilsson, *A History of Greek Religion*, New York, 1964.

31. Otto, op. cit., p. 209.

32. Lévi-Strauss, *Anthropologie structurale*, p. 232, and *Du Miel au cendres*, p. 362.

33. Max Müller, *Collected Works: Chips from a German Workshop*, Vol. 4, *Essays on Mythology and Folklore*, London, 1900, pp. 78–79, and Ernst Cassirer *Language and Myth*, trans. Susanne K. Langer, New York, n.d. [1946], p. 72 [Dover paperback].

34. H. D. F. Kitto, *Form and Meaning in Drama*, London, 1956, pp. 1–86.

35. Louis Séchan, *Etudes sur la tragédie grecque dans ses rapports avec la céramique*, Paris, 1927. T. B. L. Webster, *Art and Literature in Fourth Century Athens*, London, 1956. Denys L. Page, ed. Euripides' *Medea*, Oxford 1964 [1938], p. xxiii.

36. To be sure, Euripides has a cult introduced, if less unqualifiedly than a historical account, still no less definitely.

37. William S. Barrett, Ed., Euripides' *Hippolytos*, Oxford, 1964, p. 155.

38. Kitto, *Greek Tragedy*, p. 211. "It is quite evident once more that this is no tragedy of character."

39. Barrett, op. cit., pp. 155–56.

40. B. M. W. Knox, "The *Hippolytus* of Euripides," in *Euripides: A Collection of Critical Essays*, ed. Erich Segal, Englewood Cliffs, N.J., 1968, p.111.

41. Ibid., p. 112. " 'I gained a start on the road long ago,' πάλαι προκόψασι (23) says Aphrodite, and Artemis uses the same unusual metaphor—'And yet I shall gain nothing, and only give you pain,' καίτοι προκόψω γ' οὐδέν ἀλγυνῶ δέ σε (1297), she says to Theseus. 'I shall reveal,' δείξω (6), says Aphrodite; and Artemis says that she comes 'to reveal,' ἐκδεῖξαι (1298). 'I am not unnamed,' κοὐκ ἀνώνυμος (1), says Aphrodite, and Artemis takes up the phrase: 'not unnamed (κοὐκ ἀνώνυμος) shall Phaedra's love for you fall and be silenced.' Both of them claim, in similar words and with opposite meanings, that they reward the reverent and punish the wrongdoer (5–6 and 1339–41), and each of them, with the same characteristic word, τιμωρήσομαι (21 and 1422), announces her decision to kill the other's human protégé."

42. R. P. Winnington-Ingram, "*Hippolytus*: A Study in Causation," *Euripide, Entretiens sur l'antiquité classique*, VI, Fondation Hardt, Geneva, 1960, pp. 169–91.

43. André Rivier, in the "Discussion" of Winnington-Ingram, "*Hippolytus*:

A Study in Causation," *Entretiens*, VI, 195. "N'y a't'il pas un motif qui est donné par le mythe: le sentiment que sa mère, sa soeur, elle-même, sont la proie d'une force qui les dépasse, et qui les a prises toutes trois pour objet de son action répétée? C'est ainsi que j'entendrais le τρίτη δ' ἐγώ (v. 341) . . ."

44. Barrett, op. cit., p. 230.
45. Knox, "The *Hippolytus* of Euripides," pp. 90–91.
46. Plato burned his tragedies at the beginning of his philosophizing life. P. Friedländer, *Platon: Eidos Paideia Dialogos*, Berlin, 1928, I, 128.
47. Jean-Pierre Vernant. In a paper on Greek tragedy at a conference, "Criticism and the Sciences of Man," Johns Hopkins University, October 1966.
48. W. Nestle, *Vom Mythos sum Logos*, Stuttgart, 1942.
49. Plato, *Protagoras*, 328C. τοιοῦτόν σοι ἔφη, ὦ Σώκρατες, ἐγὼ καὶ μῦθον καὶ λόγον εἴρηκα.
50. Plato, *Gorgias*, 523A. ὅν σὺ μὲν ἡγήσῃ μῦθον, ὡς ἐγὼ οἶμαι, ἐγὼ δε λόγον.
51. Plato, *Symposium*, 218A. Alcibiades speaks of himself as δηχθεὶς ὑπὸ τῶν ἐν φιλοσοφίᾳ λογῶν, οἳ ἔχονται ἐχίδνης ἀγριώτερον.
52. The finale of *Alcestis, Andromache, Bacchae, Helen*, and, with a variation in the first line, *Medea*.
53. Plato, *Republic*, 329B, C, D.
54. Maximus of Tyre. μύθους λόγου μὲν ἀφανεστέρους, αἰνίγματος δέ σαφεστέρους.

## CHAPTER 2: THEATRON

1. Nietzsche, *Die Gebürt der Tragödie, Nietzsches Werke*, Salzburg, n.d., I, 623. "Mit dieser neuen Vision ist das Drama vollständig.

   Nach dieser Erkenntnis haben wir die griechische Tragödie als den dionysischen Chor zu verstehen, der sich immer von neuem wieder in einer apollinischen Bilderwelt entladet. Jene Chorpartien, mit denen die Tragödie durchflochten ist, sind also gewissermassen der Mutter-schoss des ganzen sogenannten Dialogs, d. h. der gesamten Bühnen-welt, des eigenlichen Dramas. Somit ist das Drama die apollinische Versinnlichung dionysischer Erkenntnisse und dadurch wie durch eine ungeheure Kluft vom Epos abgeschieden."
2. Green, *Un Oeil en trop*, Paris, 1969, p. 14.
3. Marcel Mauss, "Du Don, et en particulier de l'obligation à rendre les présents," *Sociologie et anthropologie*, Paris, 1969, pp. 145–71.
4. "A former actor of Stanislavskij's told me how at his audition he was asked by the famous director to make forty different messages from the phrase *Segodnja vecerom* 'This evening,' by diversifying its expressive tint. He made a list of some forty emotional situations, then emitted the given phrase in accordance with each of these situations . . . this actor was asked to repeat Stanislavskij's text. He wrote down some fifty situations framing the same elliptic sentence and made of it fifty corresponding messages for a tape record. Most of the messages were correctly and circumstantially decoded by Moscovite listeners. May I add that all such emotive cues easily undergo linguistic analysis?" Roman Jakobson, "Linguistics and Poetics," in *Style in Language*, ed.

Thomas A. Sebeok, Cambridge, 1960, as reprinted in S. R. Levin and S. Chatman, *Essays on the Language of Literature*, New York, 1967, p. 300.

5. Jacques Lacan, *Écrits*, Paris, 1966.

6. Ibid., "D'une question préliminaire à tout traitement possible de la psychose," pp. 531–83, and especially p. 541, "Que Freud ici nous a-t-il apporté? Nous sommes entré en matière en affirmant que pour le problème de la psychose, cet apport avait abouti à une retombée.

"Elle est immédiatement sensible dans le simplisme des ressorts qu'on invoque en des conceptions qui se ramènent toutes à ce schéma fondamental: comment faire passer l'intérieur dans l'extérieur? Le sujet en effet a beau englober ici un ça opaque, c'est tout de même en tant que *moi*, c'est-à-dire, de façon tout à fait exprimée dans l'orientation psychanalytique présente, en tant que ce même *percipiens* increvable, qu'il est invoqué dans la motivation de la psychose. Ce *percipiens* a tout pouvoir sur son corrélatif non moins inchangé: la réalité, et le modèle de ce pouvoir est pris dans une donnée accessible à l'expérience commune, celle de la projection affective."

7. Plato, *Protagoras*, 358D, E.

8. Bruno Snell, "Aischylos und das Handeln im Drama," *Philologus: Zeitschrift für das klassische Altertum*, Supplementband XX, Leipzig, 1928, p. 54. Wurde vorhin als das Charakteristische der Angst hervorgehoben, dass in ihr die Möglichkeiten des Lebens als bedroht empfunden wurden, so zeigt sich jetzt, wieviel prägnanter noch dies für den tragischen φόβος zu fassen ist: eine notwendige Zukunft steht auf dem Spiel. So ist der φόβος der Zustand einer Krise, da wir dicht vor dem Augenblick stehen, dass der Mensch selbst zu handeln, sich selbst zu entscheiden gezwungen wird, und es liegt nichts Willkürliches daren, die Frage τί δράσω; mit dem φόβος zu verbinden. Der φόβος ist der Grund, auf dem das δρᾶν nun erwachsen wird, sobald nur die unverbrüchliche Gültigkeit des einen Anspruchs ganz erfasst ist. In dem φόβος erfährt der Mensch also die Spannung zwischen dem Allgemeinen in sich und dem Nur-Persönlichen.

9. A. C. Pearson, *The Fragments of Sophocles*, Amsterdam, 1963, pp. xxviii-xxxii.

10. Scholia, as cited by Kitto, *Greek Tragedy*, pp. 123 and 129. See also A. J. A. Waldock, *Sophocles the Dramatist*, Cambridge, 1951, pp. 49–79, [1966; Cambridge paperback], and Albin Lesky, *Die Tragische Dichtung der Hellenen*, Göttingen, 1956, p. 112.

11. J. V. Cunningham, *Woe or Wonder: The Emotional Effect of Shakespearian Tragedy*, Denver, 1951, [1964; Swallow paperback].

12. Antoine Meillet, *Aperçu d'une histoire de la langue grecque*, Paris, 1920, p. 86. "Faire une cérémonie religieuse, c'est passer du domaine humain au domaine divin, sortir du monde profane et entrer dans le sacré. Pour y réussir, on est conduit à se servir d'une langue. . . . Or les langues littéraires sont souvent issues de langues religieuses."

13. Bruno Nettl, *Music in Primitive Culture*, Cambridge, Mass., 1956.

14. Jahnheinz Jahn, *Muntu*, New York, 1961 [1958], p. 39.

15. C. L. Barber, *Shakespeare's Festive Comedy*, Cleveland and New York, 1959, [1963; Meridian paperback], and Alice V. Griffin, *Pageantry on the Shakespearian Stage*, New Haven, 1951.

16. B. M. W. Knox, *Oedipus at Thebes*, Chapter II, "Athens," New Haven, 1957, pp. 53–106, and Vernant, "On Greek Tragedy," as cited.
17. George Thomson, *Greek Lyric Metre*, Cambridge, 1961 [1929].
18. Gerald Else, *The Origin and Early Form of Greek Tragedy*, Cambridge, 1967, pp. 41–42.
19. Sigmund Freud, *Gesammelte Werke*, XIII, London, 1955 [1940], p. 28. "Wir haben erfahren, dass die unbewussten Seelenvorgänge an sich 'zeitlos' sind. Das heisst zunächst, dass sie nicht zeitlich geordnet werden, dass die Zeit nichts an ihnen verändert, dass man die Zeitvorstellung nicht an sie heranbringen kann. Es sind dies negative Charaktere, die man sich nur durch Vergleichung mit den bewussten seelischen Prozessen deutlich machen kann."
20. Herodotus, 5. 67. 5 πρὸς τὰ πάθεα . . . τραγικοῖσι χοροῖσι ἐγέραιρον.
21. Plato, *Philebus*, 48A.

        Σω.   καὶ μὴν καὶ τάς γε τραγικὰς θεωρήσεις,
              ὅταν ἅμα χαίροντες κλάωσι, μέμνησαι;
        Πρω.  τί δ' οὔ;
        Σω.   τὴν δ' ἔν ταῖς κωμῳδίαις διάθεσιν
              ἡμῶν τῆς ψυχῆς, ἆρ οἶσθ' ὡς ἔστι
              κἂν τούτοις μεῖξις λύπης τε καὶ ἡδονῆς;

22. George Thomson, *Aeschylus and Athens*, London, 1967, p. 113.
23. Werner Jaeger, *Paidea*, I, Book II, Chapter II, New York, 1939, [1965; Galaxy paperback].
24. That Aristotle, in Else's reading (*Aristotle's Poetics*, pp. 224–32), meant an effect in the actor, does not close the possibility of either taking him the other way, or simply expanding his idea.
25. John D. Beazley, *Attic Red-Figure Vase Painters*, Oxford, 1963.
26. Augustus Nauck, *Tragicorum Graecorum Fragmenta*, Supplementum adiecit Bruno Snell, Hildesheim, 1964, p. 614.
27. On this disputed point, the evidence for the ignorance of the Greek spectators is weak. See A. W. Pickard-Cambridge, *The Dramatic Festivals of Athens*, rev. John Gould and D. M. Lewis, Oxford, 1968, pp. 275–76.
28. These may also be spoken in the formally different fashion of παρακαταλογή, to the accompaniment of the flute, Pickard-Cambridge, *The Dramatic Festivals of Athens*, p. 159.
29. Kitto, *Greek Tragedy*, p. 321.
30. A. M. Dale, *The Lyric Metres of Greek Drama*, Cambridge, 1948, p. 41.
31. The presence of sacrifice itself, though mythic and not hypermythic, permits the attribution of still another structuring of mythic patterns, that of René Girard ("Symétrie et dissymétrie dans le mythe d'Oedipe," *Critique*, 24 [February 1968]), who posits a reciprocity in hybris, where the "scapegoat" of other formulations that bring the "goat" in "goatsong" (trag-oidia) to the fore, permits the doubled other, the "brother" in a literal or metaphoric sense, to transpose his own hybris through another. All social actions, Girard says, are reciprocal except sacrifice, which channels its effect off one way, towards the gods; because a sacrifice, literal or metaphorical, permits the recognition of violence by

positing violence without the *dike* of just retaliation, and may be seen to underscore the total reciprocity of exchange patterns in society by abrogating them in a unique and universal instance.

While a bull, a pig, some flowers, and not a goat (Pickard-Cambridge op. cit., pp. 61–67) were sacrificed before the performance at the Greater Dionysia, this pattern, like Murray's of the year-god, may be accepted as a semantic element in the Greek tragic structure, to describe in mythic terms the formalized reciprocity of the two actors with or without the mediating third. And it may also transpose the primitive element in tragedy into a model for the audience's life. But like all such patterns, to make it paramount and finally resolving would effectually abrogate the uniqueness of an individual tragedy by annulling the transformations its *logoi* had performed upon (this or another) *mythos*.

## CHAPTER 3: ATE

1. Jacques Lacan, *Ecrits*, Paris, 1966, p. 623.
2. Ibid., p. 691.
3. William S. Barrett, ed., Euripides' *Hippolytos*, Oxford, 1964, p. 206.
4. Michel Foucault, *Histoire de la folie à l'âge classique*, Paris, 1961.
5. E. R. Dodds, *The Greeks and the Irrational*, Berkeley, 1963 [1951], p. 64.
6. Henry George Liddell and Robert Scott, *A Greek-English Lexicon*, rev. Henry Stuart Jones, Oxford, 1966 [1940], *sub voc.*
7. F. M. Cornford, *Thucydides Mythistoricus*, London, 1907.
8. Brooks Otis elaborates this point in a book in progress on Roman civilization.
9. Herodotus, III, 40–42. For this version, *The Histories*, trans. Aubrey de Sélincourt, Baltimore, 1954, [1961; Penguin paperback], pp. 191–93.
10. Ibid., III. 125; pp. 225–26.
11. Plato, *Gorgias*, 470E, 8–10.

> ΠΩΛ. τί δέ; ἐν τούτῳ ἡ πᾶσα εὐδαιμονία ἐστίν;
> ΣΩ.  "Ως γε ἐγὼ λέγω, ὦ Πῶλε· τὸν μὲν γὰρ
> καλὸν καὶ ἀγαθὸν ἄνδρα καὶ γυναῖκα
> εὐδαίμονα εἶναί φημι, τὸν δὲ ἄδικον
> καὶ πονηρὸν ἄθλιον

12. Aristotle, *Poetics*, 1453a, 10. καὶ ὁ Εὐριπίδης εἰ καὶ τὰ ἄλλα μὴ εὖ οἰκονομεῖ ἀλλὰ τραγικώτατός γε τῶν ποιητῶν φαίνεται.
13. Hans Diller, "Umwelt und Masse als dramatische Faktoren bei Euripides," *Euripide, Entretiens sur l'antiquité classique*, VI, Fondation Hardt, Geneva, 1960, p. 3.
14. Claude Lévi-Strauss, *La Pensée sauvage*, Paris, 1962, pp. 165–66.
15. The word is repeated by Heracles (576) and again by Amphitryon himself (718).
16. H. D. F. Kitto, *Greek Tragedy*, Garden City, N.Y., 1952, [1954; Anchor Books ed.], p. 256. "We are told (a) that Heracles did go to Hades and did find Cerberus; (b) that Cerberus is left at Hermione (a natural place, as it was the seat of a chthonian cult, and of an entrance to Hades); (c) that Eurystheus, far from possessing Cerberus, does not yet know of Heracles' return from Hades; and (d) that Heracles was so

long in Hades because he added to his original mission the rescue of Theseus. Theseus is not indeed still with him, having gone home to Athens.

"If we accept the story at all, these details, and the interruption of the action that they entail, are easily explicable; (a) is wanted to prepare for Theseus' arrival at the end of the play, (b) is wanted to explain (c), which is itself necessary for the madness-scene, where Heracles imagines himself to be at Argos attacking Eurystheus. This visit to Argos is very much on his mind."

17. E. M. Blaiklock, *The Male Characters of Euripides*, Chapter VII, "The Epileptic," Wellington, 1952, pp. 122–40.
18. Ulrich von Wilamowitz-Moellendorff, *Euripides Herakles*, Berlin, 1959, [1895] II, 109 ff.

## CHAPTER 4: TELOS

1. Remy Kwant, *Phenomenology of Language*, Pittsburgh, 1965, pp. 162, 164, 165, 231.
2. This and other meanings of *telos* are elaborated by Ulrich Fischer, *Der Telosgedanke in den Dramen des Aischylos*, Hildesheim, 1965.
3. John J. Finley, Jr., *Pindar and Aeschylus*, Cambridge, Mass., 1955, p. 181.
4. Bruno Snell, "Aischylos und das Handeln im Drama," *Philologus: Zeitschrift für das klassische Altertum*, Supplementband XX, Leipzig, 1928. Snell demonstrates that the diction of this concluding scene argues for its authenticity.
5. Richard Y. Hathorn, *Tragedy, Myth, and Mystery*, Bloomington, 1962, [1966; Midland paperback].
6. Wolfgang Kiefner, *Der Religiöse Allbegriff des Aischylos*, Hildesheim, 1965.
7. *Aeschylus*, Vol. II, "Appendix," ed. Hugh Lloyd Jones, Loeb Classical Library, Cambridge, Mass., 1963, Fragment 25, p. 395.
8. Nauck, Fragments 196 and 199, p. 418–49.
9. Eduard Fraenkel, *Aeschylus: Agamemnon*, Oxford, 1962 [1950], II, 39.
10. Bruno Snell, *Dichtung und Gesellschaft*, Hamburg, 1965, p. 164. "Immer wieder tauchen hier komposita mit συν—auf: so wichtig ist der Gedanke des Zusammenseins, des gemeinsamen Tuns und Empfindens."
11. Jacques Lacan, *Écrits*, "L'instance de la lettre dans l'inconscient," Paris, 1966, pp. 493–528.
12. Finley, *Pindar and Aeschylus*, p. 249.
13. Aristotle, *Poetics*, 1458a.
14. *The Odes of Pindar*, trans, Richmond Lattimore, Chicago, 1947, [1959; Phoenix Books], p. 43.
15. Denys L. Page, ed., Euripides' *Medea*, Oxford, 1964 [1938], ad loc., 401–6.
16. A. S. Cook, *Prisms: Studies in Modern Literature*, Chapter V, "Action," Bloomington and London, 1967, pp. 128–47.
17. Max Hermann, *Die Entstehung der berufsmässigen Schauspielkunst im Altertum und in der Neuzeit*, Berlin, 1962. "[Eine] Bindung von Übermenschtum und Aberglauben." "Ein grossartiges Unternehmen das gleicherweise von einem kuhnem Geist wie von einer leidenschaftlichen Sehnsucht zeugt."

18. Wolfgang Schadewaldt, *Monolog und Selbstgesprach*, Berlin, 1966, pp. 38–46.
19. John A. Peradotto, "Kledonomancy in the Oresteia," *A. J. P.*, Jan. 1969, pp. 1–69.
20. Jebb, *Sophocles Trachiniae*, Amsterdam, 1962, XX-XXI.
21. Plato, *Phaedo*, 58b.
22. George Thomson, *The Oresteia of Aeschylus*, Amsterdam and Prague, 1966, II, 142. "In the dark underworld, where all things are reversed ... mourning, in its usual form of eulogy of the dead man ... is joy to him ... ; and so such mourning commonly bears the name of χάριτες.

   ... Orestes fears, therefore, that such mourning, instead of rousing Agamemnon, will only please and comfort him; for, just as darkness is the reverse of light, so will mourning appear as comfort to the dead."

   Gilbert Murray, *Euripides and His Age*, London, 1918, p. 97 [1965; Oxford paperback]. "But there is one thought which often recurs in Euripides in plays of all periods, and is specially thrown in his teeth by Aristophanes. That satirist, when piling up Euripides' theatrical iniquities, takes as his comic climax 'women who say Life is not Life'. The reference is to passages like fr. 833, from the *Phrixus*:
   Who knows if this thing called dying is living,
   And living is dying? And yet of mortal men
   Those who see are sick, and those who have perished
   Are not sick, nor do they perform evil things. [my translation.]
   (Cf. fr. 638, 816; also *Helena*, 1013; *Frogs*, 1082, 1477). The idea recurs again and again, as also does the thought that death is 'some other shape of life' in the *Medea* and even in the *Ion* (*Med.*, 1039; *Ion*, 1068). Nay, more, death may be the state that we unconsciously long for, and that really fulfils our inmost desires: 'There is no rest on this earth,' says a speaker in the *Hippolytus* (191 f.)."
23. Nauck, Fragment 638, p. 560.

## CHAPTER 5: NOMOS

1. Jean Pierre Vernant, *Les Origines de la pensée grecque*, Paris, 1962, p. 118.
2. Lévi-Strauss, *Le Cru et le cuit*, Paris, 1964, p. 119.
3. Jacqueline de Romilly, *Time in Greek Tragedy*, Ithaca, 1968, p. 4.
4. Aristotle, *Poetics*, 1452b, 12. μέρη δὲ τραγῳδίας ... κεχωρισμένα τάδε ἐστίν, πρόλογος ἐπεισόδιον ἔξοδος χορικόν, καὶ τούτου τὸ μὲν πάροδος τὸ δὲ στάσιμον· κοινὰ μὲν ἁπάντων ταῦτα, ἴδια δὲ τὰ ἀπὸ τῆς σκηνῆς καὶ κόμμοι.
5. William Arrowsmith, from "The Criticism of Greek Tragedy," *Oedipus Rex: A Mirror for Greek Drama*, ed. A. S. Cook, Belmont, Calif., 1963, pp. 155–69.
6. Ignacio Errandonea, S. J., *Sofocles: Investigaciones sobre la estructura dramatica de sus siete tragedias y sobre la personalidad de sus coros*, Madrid, 1968, p. 175.
7. H. D. F. Kitto, *Sophocles: Dramatist and Philosopher*, London, 1958, p. 7.
8. Charles P. Segal, "The *Electra* of Sophocles," *Transactions and Proceedings of the American Philological Association*, 97, (1966) 475–76.
9. Ibid., pp. 531–32. Segal is here himself using Thomas M. Woodward,

"*Electra* by Sophocles: The Dialectical Design," *HSCP*, 68 (1964) 163–205.
10. A. J. A. Waldock, *Sophocles the Dramatist*, Cambridge, 1951, p. 186 [1966; Cambridge paperback].
11. Segal, op. cit., p. 476–77.
12. Errandonea, op. cit., p. 129.
13. Werner Jaeger, classroom lecture, February, 1946.
14. G. W. F. Hegel, *Aesthetik*, Frankfurt, 1957 [1842], II, 560–69.
15. B. M. W. Knox, *The Heroic Temper: Studies in Sophoclean Tragedy*, Berkeley, 1966, p. 117.
16. Antoine Meillet, *Aperçu d'une histoire de la langue grecque*, Paris, 1920, p. 140.
17. H. A. Pohlsander, *Metrical Studies in the Lyrics of Sophocles*, Leiden, 1964, pp. 25–26. Pohlsander tends to analyze the doubled meters of *epiploke* into the more complex of the two combined forms, but anapests, as the staple of early tragedy, are surely always heard when they enter into combination.
18. A. M. Dale, *The Lyric Metres of Greek Drama*, Cambridge, 1948, p. 129.
19. Gerhart Müller, "Chor und Handlung bei den griechischen Tragikern," *Sophocles*, ed. Hans Diller, Darmstadt, 1967.
20. Knox, *The Heroic Temper*, p. 110, citing lines 484–85, 525, 678–80 740, 746, 756.
21. Walter Jens, "*Antigone*-Interpretationen," *Sophocles*, ed. Hans Diller, p. 299.
22. Walther Kranz, *Stasimon*, Berlin, 1933, p. 196.
23. Knox, *The Heroic Temper*, pp. 78, 84.
24. Dale, op. cit., p. 172.

## CHAPTER 6: THEOS

1. Heraclitus, Fragment 119, Diels-Kranz v.I, p. 177. E. R. Dodds, *The Greeks and the Irrational*, p. 182, makes virtually the same point.
2. Heraclitus, Fragment 62, Diels-Kranz v.I, p. 165. ἀθάνατοι θνητοί, θνητοὶ ἀθάνατοι, ζῶντες τὸν ἐκείνων θάνατον, τὸν δὲ ἐκείνων βίον τεθνεῶτες.
3. H. D. F. Kitto, "The Idea of God in Aeschylus and Sophocles," *La Notion du divin depuis Homère jusqu'à Platon, Entretiens sur l'antiquité classique*, I, Fondation Hardt, Berne, 1955, p. 189.
4. J. Harrison, *Themis: A Study of the Social Origins of Greek Religion*, 2nd ed., 1963 [1927], pp. 113–18.
5. Nauck, Fragment 151, p. 403.
6. René Girard, "Symétrie et dissymétrie dans le mythe d'Oedipe," *Critique*, 24 (February 1968).
7. Knox, *The Heroic Temper*, p. 84.
8. Nauck, Fragment 360, pp. 467–68.
9. G. Zuntz, "On Euripides' *Helena*: Theology and Irony," *Entretiens*, VI, pp. 222–23.
10. A. W. Verrall, *Euripides: The Rationalist*, Cambridge, 1913.
11. Nauck, Fragment 21, p. 369.
12. Dionysus was raised as a girl by Ino and Athamas, who got him from Zeus through Hermes. A. B. Cook, *Zeus*, 1914 [repr. 1965] I, 674, citing Apollodorus, 3, 4, 3.

13. Charles Boer, *The Language of Tragic Humor,* "The Bacchae," unpublished thesis, State University of New York at Buffalo, 1967.
14. Thomas Rosenmeyer, "Ajax: Tragedy and Time," *The Masks of Tragedy,* Austin, 1963, p. 106.

## CHAPTER: 7 DAIMON

1. Martin Foss, *Death, Sacrifice, and Tragedy,* Lincoln, Nebraska, 1966, p. 45.
2. Martin Heidegger, *Sein und Zeit,* Tübingen, 1963, [1928], p. 317.
3. Knox, *Oedipus at Thebes,* pp. 5–9.
4. Cook, *Oedipus Rex: A Mirror for Greek Drama,* pp. 87–88.
5. Lionel Abel, "Is There a Tragic Sense of Life," *Moderns on Tragedy,* New York, 1967. [Fawcett paperback].
6. Knox, *Oedipus at Thebes,* p. 47.
7. Girard, "Symetrie et dissymetrie dans le mythe d'Oedipe."
8. Ibid., p. 114.
9. Ibid., p. 133.
10. Thalia Phillies Howe, "Taboo in the Oedipus Theme," *Transactions and Proceedings of the American Philological Association,* 93 (1962), 143.
11. As William Moebius says (unpublished dissertation, State University of New York at Buffalo, 1969, p. 74), "if the *persona* can engage the *power* of the objects around him on his behalf, and the power of things underneath and beyond him, calling upon our imagination to accept his roll-call as the ultimate census of our own, his personality ceases to be theatrical, a familiar copy of someone we know, an animation of our contingent world, and becomes endowed with a holiness that we know only in certain half-awake moments."

# INDEX OF NAMES

# INDEX OF PLAYS